ENGLISH FOR ACADEMICS

A communication skills course for tutors, lecturers and PhD students

In collaboration with the British Council

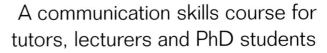

BOOK 1

CAMBRIDGE
UNIVERSITY PRESS

University Printing House, Cambridge CB2 8BS, United Kingdom

Cambridge University Press is part of the University of Cambridge.

It furthers the University's mission by disseminating knowledge in the pursuit of education, learning and research at the highest international levels of excellence.

www.cambridge.org
Information on this title: www.cambridge.org/9781107434769

© Cambridge University Press and the British Council Russia 2014

It is normally necessary for written permission to be obtained *in advance* from a publisher. Some pages in this book are designed to be copied and distributed in class. The normal requirements are waived here and it is not necessary to write to Cambridge University Press for permission for an individual teacher to make copies for use within his or her own classroom. Only those pages that carry the wording ' © Cambridge University Press' may be copied.

First published 2014

Printed in Poland by Opolgraf

A catalogue record for this publication is available from the British Library

ISBN 978-1-107-43476-9 Book with online audio

Additional resources for this publication at www.cambridge.org/elt/english-for-academics

Cambridge University Press has no responsibility for the persistence or accuracy of URLs for external or third-party internet websites referred to in this publication, and does not guarantee that any content on such websites is, or will remain, accurate or appropriate.

Contents

Map Reading — 4

Map Listening — 5

Map Speaking — 6

Map Writing — 7

Introduction — 8

Module 1 Reading — 9

Module 2 Listening — 59

Module 3 Speaking — 93

Module 4 Writing — 131

Academic vocabulary — 169

Acknowledgements — 174

Map Reading

Module 1 Reading   9

Unit 1 International academic conferences   10

Lesson 1 Conference announcements   10

Lesson 2 Calls for papers   14

Lesson 3 Academic and professional events   18

Unit 2 University teaching, learning and research   22

Lesson 1 Teaching and learning at higher education institutions   22

Lesson 2 Virtual learning environments   28

Lesson 3 University research   32

Unit 3 Academic publications   38

Lesson 1 Publishing matters   38

Lesson 2 Popular science articles   43

Lesson 3 Research reports   46

Unit 4 International cooperation   51

Lesson 1 International cooperation programmes   51

Lesson 2 Grants   54

Map Listening

Module 2 Listening   59

Unit 1 Attending a conference   60
Lesson 1 Arrival   60
Lesson 2 Welcome to the Grand Hotel   63
Lesson 3 I seem to have a problem   65

Unit 2 Troubleshooting   67
Lesson 1 Is there any technical help?   67
Lesson 2 Are you in charge?   70
Lesson 3 Is the problem solved?   72
Lesson 4 Good news ... Bad news   74

Unit 3 Networking   76
Lesson 1 Have we met before?   76
Lesson 2 What did you think of it?   78
Lesson 3 What we'll do ...   80
Lesson 4 Can we talk?   82

Unit 4 In the audience   84
Lesson 1 Your participation is welcome   84
Lesson 2 The three golden rules   87
Lesson 3 A story to illustrate my point   89
Lesson 4 And finally ...   91

Map Speaking

Module 3 Speaking — 93

Unit 1 Socialising — 94
Lesson 1 Greetings and introductions — 94
Lesson 2 Starting and keeping a conversation going — 97
Lesson 3 Showing interest and reacting to news — 99
Lesson 4 Inviting — 101
Lesson 5 Paying and receiving compliments — 103
Lesson 6 Saying thank you, sorry and goodbye — 105

Unit 2 Presentation skills — 107
Lesson 1 What makes a good presentation — 107
Lesson 2 Developing presentation skills — 111
Lesson 3 Working with visuals — 117
Lesson 4 Your presentation skills — 121

Role-play activities — 123
Learner A — 123
Learner B — 126

Forms — 129

Slides checklist — 129

Feedback form — 130

Map Writing

Module 4 Writing   131

Unit 1 Academic correspondence   132

Lesson 1 Ready to start   132

Lesson 2 A reference letter   135

Lesson 3 Proposal for partnership   137

Lesson 4 Writing a cover letter for a grant proposal   140

Unit 2 Writing a summary   142

Lesson 1 What makes a good summary?   142

Lesson 2 Topic sentences   145

Unit 3 Writing an abstract   147

Lesson 1 Make your abstract cohesive   147

Lesson 2 Abstracts from different fields of study   151

Unit 4 Writing an executive summary of a grant proposal   155

Lesson 1 A grant proposal   155

Lesson 2 Polishing an executive summary   159

Unit 5 Describing visual data   163

Lesson 1 Visual information   163

Lesson 2 Writing about trends   166

Introduction

Did you know that most communication in English around the world takes place between non-native speakers using English as a *lingua franca*? This is very often the case when academics communicate with each other within their specialisms.

If you are attending classes to improve your English in order to take part in international communication in your academic field, this coursebook is intended for you. It deals with topics and situations that you will find relevant and helpful, such as:

- presentation skills
- academic correspondence
- conference announcements and calls for papers
- grant proposals
- reading and writing abstracts
- understanding lectures and discussions
- social situations, e.g. interaction with colleagues from other countries, or making travel and accommodation arrangements

To get started, you will need to have a lower-intermediate level of English (equivalent to B1 on the Common European Framework of Reference). The book focuses on communication through the four skills of Listening, Speaking, Reading and Writing, and in class time you will be involved in challenging tasks and interesting activities together with your fellow learners. But please remember that you will also need to make time to work outside class hours in order to make significant progress in English.

Be ready to experiment with your English. It doesn't matter if you make some mistakes – nobody is perfect!

Reading

module 1

In this module you will:

- read a range of common academic tests

- develop your ability to read confidently and efficiently

Unit 1 International academic conferences

By the end of this unit you will be able to

⇒ scan conference programmes for relevant information

⇒ identify the main point or important information

⇒ guess the meaning of unknown words from context

⇒ understand and use the vocabulary of conference announcements

Lesson 1 Conference announcements

Lead-in

1 Work in groups and discuss the questions. Then briefly tell the class what you have learned.

1 How often do you take part in international conferences? Have you ever given a presentation at one? If yes, in which language did you present?
2 Where do you usually get information about conferences?
3 When you read a conference announcement, what information do you look for first?

Reading focus

2 Look at the titles of five conferences (A–E). Which would be interesting to the following people?

1 a biologist
2 a data-protection expert
3 an MBA lecturer

A 2nd International Conference on Environmental Pollution and Remediation

B World Congress on Internet Security

C Culture, Mind, and Brain: Emerging Concepts, Methods, Applications

D Cultures of Decolonisation: 1945–1970

E Third Annual Academic Conference on Social Responsibility
Sustainability: Issues and Strategies

3 Check the meaning of the words/phrases in bold. Then answer the questions.

Which of the conference titles

1 may **relate to** conference(s) dealing with health issues?
2 seem(s) like an announcement of a **regular event**?
3 **address(es) issues** connected with a specific period of time?

4 **Look quickly at this text and answer the questions.**

1 What is its purpose?
2 What information can you get from it?
3 What types of words (e.g. articles) are missing?
4 Can you work out the general meaning based only on the content words?

_____ IADIS e-Learning 2013 conference aims _____ address _____ main issues _____ concerns _____ e-Learning.

_____ conference covers _____ technical _____ non-technical aspects _____ e-Learning. Main topics _____ identified. However, innovative contributions _____ don't fit into these areas _____ also be considered _____ they might be _____ benefit _____ conference attendees.

Acceptance _____ based primarily _____ originality, significance _____ quality _____ contribution.

5 **Skim the following announcements focusing on content words and match them with three of the conference titles from Activity 2.**

1 Title: _____

Location: California, USA
Date: 19–20 October 2013

The aim of this two-day conference is to highlight emerging concepts, methodologies and applications in the study of culture, the mind and the brain, paying particular attention to:
- cutting-edge neuroscience research that is successfully incorporating culture and the social world;
- the context in which methods are used as well as the assumptions that shape research questions; and
- the kinds and quality of collaborations that can advance interdisciplinary research training.
email: cmb@cmb135.org

2 Title: _____

Host: McGill University, International ASET Inc.
Organisers: International ASET Inc.
Deadline for abstracts: 15 March 2013

ICEPR is a series of international conferences held yearly. These conferences focus on all aspects of Environmental Science, Engineering, and Technology. After successfully holding the first ICEPR in Ottawa (Canada), International ASET Inc. will be hosting the next conference in Montreal. The aim of ICEPR '13 is to bring together the Canadian and international communities working in the field of environmental sciences, engineering and technology, and to foster an environment conducive to recent advances in this field. This conference will also provide a golden opportunity to develop new collaborations and gather world experts on the different topics including pollution detection, environmental remediation and pollution prevention. Through the 2nd conference, a great opportunity to share knowledge and expertise will be created, taking advantage of the synergy of the 1st conference. The ICEPR '13 program will include invited keynote talks, oral presentation sessions, and poster sessions.
Email: icepr2013@icepr489.com

3 Title: _____

> **Location: Ontario, Canada**
> **Date: 6 October 2013**
>
> WorldCIS-2013 is an international forum dedicated to the advancement of the theory and practical implementation of security on the internet and computer networks. The inability to properly secure computer networks against emerging threats and vulnerabilities, and sustaining privacy and trust, have been a key focus of research.
>
> Email: info@wcis396.org
> Visit the website at www.wcis396.org

6 Look again at the conference announcements in Activity 5 and complete the table.

Announcement	Location	Theme/Purpose	Organisers	Contact
1				
2				
3				

7 Answer the questions about the three announcements.

1 What is the last possible date for sending a summary of your research to one of these conferences?
2 Which conference(s) focus(es) on challenges presented by the development of technology?
3 Which event is part of a conference chain (more than one event on the same topic)?
4 In which city does the 2nd International Conference take place?
5 Which announcement mentions the length of the conference? What is it?

Vocabulary focus

8 Find the following words in the conference announcements. What parts of speech (nouns or verbs) are they in the texts?

> advance   share   shape   focus   host   study   trust   aim   highlight   research

9 Complete the sentences with words from Activity 8. First, decide which part of speech it should be. In one sentence, more than one answer is possible.

1 Glasgow University's Centre for Drug Prevention Studies is to _____ a conference on 20 April, aimed at assessing new rehabilitation methods.
2 Professor Samuelsson's talk has to be the _____ of this year's forum.
3 The _____ of cross-cultural differences in the development of research methods, nomenclature and research organisation between different national and geographical traditions is our first objective.
4 Other factors, like the institutional need to _____ knowledge, to publish, to engage in research, and to generate performance indicators, would remain challenges for modern academia.
5 The _____ of this sign proves its hieroglyphic origin.
6 Schools must get regular feedback from the communities they _____ to serve.

10 Match the words (1–7) with the correct definition of the word as it is used in the announcements in Activity 5.

1 session
  a a formal meeting or series of meetings of an organisation such as a parliament or a law court
  b a period of time or meeting arranged for a particular activity

2 key
  a a piece of metal that is used for opening or closing a lock, starting a car engine, etc. (noun)
  b any of the set of controls that you press with your fingers on a computer or musical instrument to produce letters, numbers or musical notes (noun)
  c very important and having a lot of influence on other people or things (adj.)

3 to hold
  a to take and keep something in your hand or arms
  b to believe an idea or opinion
  c to make something, especially a meeting or an election, happen
  d to have something, especially a position or money, or to control something

4 culture
  a ways of working that are typical of an organisation
  b the ways of life, customs and beliefs of a group of people
  c activities involving music and the arts
  d the act of growing crops

5 forum
  a a situation or meeting in which people can talk about a problem or matter especially of public interest
  b a place on the internet where people can leave messages or discuss particular subjects with other people

6 to advance
  a to go or move something forward
  b to pay someone some money before the regular time
  c to develop or improve something

7 particular
  a special, great
  b specific, this and no other
  c demanding that close attention should be given to every detail

Follow-up

11 On the internet, find a short conference announcement, and save it. Delete all service words (articles, prepositions, etc.) from the text, as in Activity 4.

12 Work in pairs. Give each other your gapped texts and try to complete them. Was it difficult to do? Why/Why not?

Lesson 2 Calls for papers

Lead-in

1 Look at these expressions with the word *paper*. Which ones have the same meaning of *paper* as in the title?

1 to paper walls
2 a paper on nanotechnology
3 to recycle paper
4 a paper outline

5 a foreign policy paper
6 paper money
7 to submit a paper
8 a paper document

Reading focus

2 Make sure you understand the meaning of these words and phrases from a call for papers.

- to provide a platform
- to submit papers
- areas of research
- registration fee
- to announce

- interdisciplinary
- welcome contributions
- take place
- abstracts

3 Work in pairs. Where do you think the words and phrases in Activity 2 will appear in a call for papers?

a near the beginning
b in the main part
c near the end

I think 'to provide a platform' will appear near the beginning because it will explain the aim of the conference.

4 Complete the text below with words and phrases from Activity 2. How many of your predictions were correct?

First International Young Scholars Symposium
Discourse, Ideology and Society (DIS)
Organised by the Discourse and Culture Academic Society (DISCAS)
Łódź, Poland, 18–20 March 2014
Call for papers deadline: 10 September 2013
First Circular – Call for Papers

We would like ¹_____ that the first international young scholars symposium on *Discourse, Ideology and Society* will ²_____ in Łódź, Poland, on 18–20 March 2014. Our goal is ³_____ where young researchers can share their expertise, interests and passion for discourse and its multiple social, political, and cultural contexts.

This ⁴_____ conference intends to explore the notion of discourse as socially constituted, historically shaped and ideologically conditioned, and to promote multidisciplinarity and integration across various fields of discourse and representation-related research. Bridging the gap between qualitative and quantitative approaches, we want to look for new solutions and tools that will allow us to cope with methodological challenges and will make it possible to address the discourse-society dialectics in a novel and comprehensive way.

We [5]_____ from all of the following areas: linguistics, sociology, political studies, psychology, journalism and media studies, advertising, culture studies and business communication. The contributions of BA, MA and PhD students and young researchers are particularly encouraged. Possible [6]_____ include, but are by no means limited to, the following:

- perspectives on discourse and communication
- qualitative and quantitative methodologies in discourse studies
- political discourse and communication
- stereotypes and discrimination in discourse
- discourse, ideology and conflict
- persuasion, manipulation and propaganda
- business and corporate communication
- advertising discourse
- visual communication

Confirmed keynote speakers
- Professor Piotr Staskowsky
- Dr Christopher Hook
- Professor Jason Gardener

Abstract submission
Papers will be allocated 20 minutes plus 10 minutes for questions. The language of the conference is English. [7]_____ of no more than 350 words (excluding references) should be sent by email as a Word attachment to conference@FIYSS.pl by 4 November 2013. Please include your name, affiliation, email address and paper title in the body of the email. Notification of acceptance decisions will be communicated via email by 10 January 2014.

Proceedings
Presenters will be invited [8]_____ based on the general theme for publication in a post-conference volume. A selection of papers will also be published in *Łódź Papers in Pragmatics* in printed and electronic formats.

Registration
The [9]_____ covers a set of conference materials, coffee breaks with refreshments and access to internet facilities. The regular fee is €70. Participants from Poland, East European countries and other developing states (please contact the organisers to check if you qualify) will be offered a reduced fee of €40 (160 PLN, conference fee). Fees should be transferred by 11 March 2014 to **this** bank account.

5 Read another call for papers and put paragraphs A–E in the correct order.

> **Mid-Atlantic Conference on British Studies**
> **Location:** Pennsylvania, US
> **Call for Papers Date:** 2013–08–21

A ☐

> We welcome participation by scholars of history, literature, anthropology, art, politics and related fields. We will accept complete panel proposals as well as individual paper proposals if they can be integrated into a viable panel.

B ☐

> The Mid-Atlantic Conference on British Studies will hold its annual meeting on 21–22 April 2014 at Pennsylvania State University, Abington. The Abington Campus is located in suburban Philadelphia 12 miles from the city centre. It is connected by road and rail links to central Philadelphia.

C ☐

> Proposals should include a brief (no more than 250 words) abstract of the paper and a curriculum vitae. Full panel proposals should also include a concise description of the panel's overall aim and indicate which panel member will serve as the primary contact.

D ☐

> All submissions must be received by 20 December 2013. Please submit proposals via email to: Dept. of History, College of William and Mary.

E ☐

> The MACBS, an affiliate of the NACBS, solicits proposals for panels and papers on Britain, the British Atlantic World, and the British Empire broadly defined.

6 Look again at the texts in Activities 4 and 5.

1 Which of them include(s) the following?
   a contact details
   b subtopics
   c deadline for submission of proposals
   d keynote speakers
   e registration fee details
2 Where are you most likely to find these calls for papers?

7 Answer the questions about the two texts.

1 Why are the 'call for papers' dates written in different ways: *2013-08-21* and *10 September 2013*?
2 How can you get to the Mid-Atlantic Conference venue (site) from downtown Philadelphia?
3 Can an American scholar attending the symposium in Poland be eligible for a reduced fee?
4 What does *MACBS* stand for? Can you guess the meaning of the N in *NACBS*?
5 When will the Young Scholars' Symposium applicants learn if their papers have been selected?
6 What two types of proposal can you submit to the Mid-Atlantic Conference on British Studies?
7 What information do you have to include if you submit a panel proposal to *MACBS*?
8 What kind of participants are especially welcome at the conference in Poland?

Vocabulary focus

8 Match words 1–7 to words a–g to form conference-related collocations. Try to do it without looking at the texts.

1 keynote	**a** conference
2 submit	**b** speakers
3 curriculum	**c** attachment
4 an interdisciplinary	**d** vitae
5 a call for	**e** an annual meeting
6 a Word	**f** papers
7 hold	**g** a proposal

9 Complete the gaps with prepositions. Sometimes there is more than one possible answer. Then check your answers in the texts.

1 submit proposals _____ email
2 organised _____ the Discourse and Culture Academic Society
3 the Mid-Atlantic Conference _____ British studies
4 based _____ the general theme
5 _____ printed and electronic formats
6 bridging the gap _____ qualitative and quantitative approaches
7 to cope _____ methodological challenges
8 fees should be transferred _____ 11 March 2014

Follow-up

10 Search online for a conference related to your subject or research area.

11 Present details of the conference to the class and explain your choice. Why does the conference or call for papers appeal to you (e.g. the topic, research or publication opportunities, keynote speakers)?

Lesson 3 Academic and professional events

Lead-in

1 Look at the list of academic and professional events. Which of them take place online and which involve face-to-face interaction?

- an e-conference
- a video conference
- a round table
- a webinar
- a forum
- a summer school (university)

Reading focus 1

2 Look quickly through Texts A–D. Complete them with the types of professional events below. There is one event you do not need.

- a summer school
- a webinar
- a round table
- an e-conference
- a forum

A

ICNC's Academic [1]_____ are a series of online talks and visual presentations on critical ideas, cases, and questions related to civil resistance and nonviolent movements. They are intended for general learners, students, and interested professionals.

These hour-long [2]_____ are offered bi-weekly, typically on Thursdays from 12–1 p.m. EST. Scholars deliver 30–40 minute presentations, which are followed by a 20–30 minute question-and-answer session. Preliminary readings may also be recommended prior to the presentation and will be sent in advance to those who register for the [3]_____ .

B

Date: 29–31 March 2014
Venue: Hotel Aerostar, Moscow

The [4]_____ will feature: plenary talks and discussions, practical workshops, discussion groups, open space, online coverage and much more.

If you are interested in speaking at the [5]_____ , please complete the speaker proposal form and return it to elisp22@ristuu.ru by 11 March.

If you would like to participate as a delegate please complete the online registration form by 25 March.

The participation in the [6]_____ is free for all registered delegates. This includes access to all sessions, welcome pack, coffee breaks and lunches.
Certificates of attendance will be provided at the end of the [7]_____ .

International delegates will need to arrange their own visas, accommodation and transport. We will be happy to provide confirmation of attendance and advice on visa and accommodation.

C

The 8_____ will take place between 27 June and 1 July, 2014 in Budapest, Hungary.

9_____ participants are expected to have at least started their graduate studies and have basic training in one of the related disciplines: either the psychological sciences / neuroscience, or in mathematics / computer science, broadly defined. The course will also be appropriate for post-docs and junior faculty.

Working knowledge of general issues in the areas of perception, memory, linear algebra, and neural networks will be useful. Undergraduates without a university degree will not be considered.

The language of the 10_____ is English; thus all applicants have to demonstrate a strong command of spoken and written English to be able to participate actively in discussions at seminars and workshops. (In some instances, short-listed applicants may be contacted for a telephone interview.)

D

Registrations are welcome from PhD students studying any aspect of substance use or misuse (or closely related topic) in any country. Participation in the 11_____ is free.

The 12_____ will run from 23 April to 27 April 2014 and will be accessible 24 hours a day. The key aims are for PhD students to learn about each other's work and to build new networks.

PhD student contributions can take the form of slide show presentations, podcasts, Word documents, audio or visual recordings (maximum file size = 10 Mb, although links can be provided to larger files hosted elsewhere, such as YouTube videos). Feel free to contribute any material relating to your research that is likely to interest others.

Video and instant-chat facilities are also available.

The 13_____ materials will be accessible to anyone who chooses to log on to the 14_____ .

3 Suggest a title for each of the events. You can look at the conference titles in Lessons 1 and 2 for help.

4 Answer these questions about the events in Activity 2.

Which event(s):

1 do(es) not involve travel expenses?
2 are the longest (five days)?
3 is/are a series of sessions?
4 may require participants to be equipped with a headset?
5 is/are face-to-face?
6 allow(s) you to participate at any time both during the day and at night?
7 offer(s) a variety of forms of participation?
8 can be viewed without registration as a participant?
9 is/are delivered in 60-minute units?

5 Work in pairs. Look again at events A–D in Activity 2. Make notes on one of the following questions. Then ask your partner questions about your information. How much can they remember?

Student A: Who can participate in the events described in Activity 2?
Student B: What are the times and lengths of each event?

6 Complete the table with names of sessions or forms of participation most typical of the following professional events. Use events A–D and examples from your own experience.

Academic conference	Webinar	Forum	E-conference	Summer school
	instant chat			

Reading focus 2

7 Look at Texts A–C below. What type of conference session do they describe?

A

> The traditional format for an input session. In this type of session, members would expect the speaker/s to spend most of the time addressing them with short periods for questions or short, focused tasks. This would normally be accompanied by a slide show presentation and a summarising handout. Members would expect to leave the session having benefited primarily from the speaker's knowledge and expertise in a specified area.

B

> These sessions can take multiple formats. One approach is to create a small group space for those interested in the same issue. This approach involves sitting in a more circular arrangement to enable greater conversation between session participants. This can aid interaction and dialogue, especially across a range of contributors. This format is designed to enable people to participate in conversation and to hear more clearly what others are saying by being able to see people's faces. This type of session works best if a clear topic is agreed upon in advance, even if it is a broad theme.

C

> At a designated time slot, presenters will be asked to stand next to their visuals and explain the content and answer questions for interested delegates. All presentations will take place at the same time and place, making for a busy and interactive area of the conference venue, which is ideal for generating discussion. Please note that your materials must be informative and must not include advertising. Presentations generally last for 45 minutes; all the materials will be on display throughout the conference and available for viewing during breaks.

8 Choose the best answer to finish each statement. Check your answers in Texts A–C in Activity 7.

1 It is inappropriate to include in a poster
   a research findings and major references.
   b any information aimed at making profit.
   c the presenter's affiliations.

2 In a paper presentation or talk, most of the speaking is done by
   a one or two carefully selected participants.
   b most of the participants in a heated discussion.
   c a chosen board of experts in the field.

3 A session that involves a number of conference participants in the discussion of a topic of fairly general interest is called
   a a talk.
   b a poster session.
   c a round table.

4 Of all the three types of session, a poster presentation is
   a the most typical of academic conferences.
   b the richest in visuals.
   c the one that needs most moderation by the chair.

5 The most valuable knowledge in a paper presentation or talk comes from
   a handouts and visual aids.
   b a lengthy opinion exchange.
   c the speaker's experience.

Vocabulary focus

9 Look at Texts A–C in Activity 7 and find adjectives which are similar in meaning to the following. Which nouns do they describe?

1 carrying the main points   *informative (materials)*
2 general, without detail
3 fixed, arranged
4 concrete, defined
5 customary, usual
6 having a narrow, specific purpose
7 crowded, with a lot of people

10 Think of a professional event you have attended recently. Describe it to a partner or the class using suitable expressions from Activity 9.

Follow-up

11 Search online for descriptions of different session types, preferably in your area of study. These are normally given on professional association sites. Share your findings with the class.

Unit 2 University teaching, learning and research

By the end of this unit you will be able to

⟹ recognise the main information in academic texts

⟹ predict what a text will be about

⟹ distinguish main ideas from supporting details

⟹ understand relations between parts of a text through the use of linking words/phrases

⟹ guess the meaning of new words/expressions from context

Lesson 1 Teaching and learning at higher education institutions

Lead-in

1 Work in pairs. Look at the list and tick the things which help you decide if an article or a book is worth reading.

in an article
- the title
- the illustrations
- the preview
- the first sentence of each paragraph

in a book
- the genre
- the author's name
- the table of contents
- the index
- the notes on the cover

Reading focus 1

2 Work in pairs. Read the titles of two articles from a postgraduate prospectus. Choose the sentences that best describe the contents.

1 'Distance-learning health courses make a world of difference.'
   a Distance education in the world is spreading.
   b Online courses in Medicine are special.
   c Online courses help people to stay healthy.

2 'Education for the real world.'
   a Universities do not always teach what students need.
   b Higher education is now easy to obtain.
   c What you study should prepare you for future work.

3 Try to predict what the articles under these titles may be about.

- Arts and minds
- In deep water

4 Quickly read the extracts (A–D) below from four different articles in the prospectus.
Match titles 1–4 to the correct extract.

1 Distance-learning health courses make a world of difference
2 Education for the real world
3 Arts and minds
4 In deep water

A

Many of us are often forced to choose between arts and science during
our education, [1]**which** can frustrate those who are fascinated with both
disciplines. Happily, the crossover between the two subject areas is
becoming more widely recognised. So, if you have an artistic talent as well
as an interest in science, there are plenty of postgraduate degrees that
combine both. 'A basic knowledge about science would help many artists
creatively,' says Mariano Molina, an Argentinian artist who is collaborating
with scientists at the University of Leicester on a project about how people
perceive art. 'Science and art have very different environments with regards
to study and work, but my advice is to be as open as you can, as [2]**both** can
be really enjoyable.'

There is no doubt that this collaborative mentality is spreading. Central Saint
Martins College of Art and Design has become the first art school in the UK
to launch an MA in Art and Science. The course, which started in September
2013, encourages students to collaborate with scientists on an in-depth
project of their choice. Suggestions have so far covered everything from
anatomy and neuroscience to gender and identity.

B

Autumn 2013 saw the launch of several distance-learning MScs, increasing
the range of online health-related courses taught by more than 50 UK
universities and medical schools. At the University of Edinburgh, the new
online MSc in Non-Communicable Diseases takes the number of online
courses offered by the College of Medicine to 15.

Dr Liz Grant, Programme Manager at the university's Global Health Academy,
explained that the decision to develop the courses came out of a recognition
that taking time out to travel to the UK for a year or two is not practical for
many health practitioners in developing countries.

'[3]**This** was a way of enabling people who are still at the coalface* to study
but continue to work,' she said. 'When someone's based in-country, it means
that they're able to be in touch with local data and apply [4]**their** learning
directly, and to learn through their work.'

who are still at the coalface = who are still working

23

C

Engineers, traditionally seen as experts in the built environment, are now turning their attention to the issue of water shortages. And there is no single cause of water scarcity, the whole water cycle – and the way we make use of it – has to be managed as sensitively and innovatively as possible. This area of engineering, known as water management, is set to become one of the coming decade's greatest challenges.

The effect of water shortages means that ongoing work can be found – and will be needed – all over the world. Peter Duffy, head of civil engineering at United Utilities, explains how water companies are experiencing a revolution. '[5]**We** have been transformed in recent years in terms of ensuring sustainability,' he says, adding that trained water professionals and academics will be essential assets to the water business, both now and in the future. 'They will play a key role in advising governments about the risk that future challenges pose, and providing solutions to [6]**these**'.

In the UK, universities have already been gearing up to meet the demand for a new generation of water experts. Postgraduates choosing [7]**this path** tend to have already studied in a related field, such as engineering, geography, biology or mathematics, but consideration is often given to those educated in unrelated subjects who can demonstrate their enthusiasm and knowledge. What is needed, universities argue, is innovative thinking and committed individuals who are prepared to join forces with the water companies, charities and organisations that are embracing the need for change.

D

Our goal in Bath is to equip students with the education and skills necessary to develop a successful career in a competitive world. We have very close relationships with industry and the public sector, [8]**which** means what we teach you and the research you undertake has relevance to the real world.

Our students are motivated and career-orientated. They understand that entry to the University of Bath is highly competitive, but they also know that as high-calibre students they are themselves in demand. We therefore strive to offer programmes that satisfy their needs and facilities that meet their expectations.

Academic life in Bath is centred on the Faculties of Engineering and Design, Humanities and Social Science; Science; and the School of Management. All our academic departments are highly active in research. [9]**This** not only benefits students undertaking research degrees, but also fosters an environment of discovery and innovation that is of benefit to all students. Learning in faculties at the cutting edge of their disciplines makes for a challenging and rewarding educational experience for students.

5 Work in pairs. Were your predictions in Activities 2 and 3 correct? Decide what influenced your interpretation of the titles.

- how carefully you read each title (e.g. 'Distance-learning health courses make a world of difference')
- how many meanings for the same words you knew (e.g. *art*)
- the use of metaphors in the title (e.g. 'In deep water')
- something else?

6 Read the article extracts again and answer the questions.

1 What do you think is the purpose of the extracts? Who are the readers?
2 Which extracts contain references to specific universities? What are their names?
3 Which extract describes a problem that requires the attention of both practitioners and universities? What is the problem?
4 Which extracts mention a variety of subjects that can be studied at that university?
5 Which extract focuses on the needs of a specific group of people? Who are they?

7 Look at words 1–9 in bold in the extracts. What does each one refer to?

1 'which' refers to 'choose between arts and science'

8 Complete the text with the following linking words.

However   for example   they   These   therefore   this

Facilitation of online discussions

Learning through online discussions is an important instructional strategy (Hung, Tan, & Chen, 2005). Research indicates that **1**_____ have numerous advantages – such as promoting students' critical thinking and knowledge construction and improving students' relationships. **2**_____, participants often do not value online discussion as an effective means of knowledge construction. Online discussion **3**_____ needs facilitation to make it more effective (Salmon, 2004). In order to achieve **4**_____ online tutors and moderators need to have appropriate skills. The literature has reported a number of specific facilitation skills that a moderator should possess, such as providing information, inviting missing students, monitoring regularly, or acknowledging contributions (see **5**_____ Barker, 2002). **6**_____ facilitation skills can be divided into four broad categories.

Vocabulary focus

9 Look at Texts A–D in Activity 4 and underline words which you can understand without a dictionary (perhaps because they also exist in your native language, e.g. *expert*).

Tip:
Some words that exist both in the English language and your mother tongue can be 'false friends'. They may sound the same, but they have different meanings (e.g. the German word *gift* means 'poison' but the English word *gift* means 'a present').

---

10 Complete the sentences with prepositions. Check your answers in Texts A–D.

1 It is important to point out that now we can make use _____ text books that were not available before.

2 The author concludes that there is continual demand from the global community _____ internet-based instruction.

3 Experts _____ the field of economics seem to have found a satisfactory solution _____ the difficulties internet start-ups face.

4 Chapter 1 introduces the topic and briefly discusses the need _____ continued research in the area of classroom interaction.

5 One of the things that students can learn _____ group work is how to interact with those who have different backgrounds and experiences.

Reading focus 2

11 Match functions 1–5 with Texts A–E. (You can match a text with more than one function.) Then explain what helped you to identify the function of the texts.

1 informing
2 inviting
3 requesting information

4 giving instructions
5 warning

A

It is important that students are respectful towards lecturers and fellow classmates, and that their behaviours do not interfere with class activities. Therefore, students are expected to adhere to the following rules when attending Marketing classes.

- Plan to arrive on time and stay for the entire class period because random arrivals and exits are disrespectful and distracting.
- All mobile phones and other electronic devices must be turned off (or set to vibrate) and hidden from view during class time.
- Laptops are allowed for note taking only (other activities such as checking emails or browsing the internet are prohibited).
- Food and beverages are NOT permitted in classrooms. Food can be consumed in designated areas only.

B

Dear Sir/Madam,

I am very interested in entering Pomona College and would appreciate you sending me the following information:

- Course Catalog
- Scholarship Information
- Financial Aid Application
- Residency Information, On-Campus and Off-Campus

Briefly, my academic career has been focused on Natural Sciences and I have consistently maintained a GPA* of 3.5. I have also successfully balanced my academic interests with athletics and work in volunteer organisations.

I look forward to hearing from you.

Faithfully,

Sam Smith

* *GPA* = Grade Point Average, quantitative measure of undergraduate academic achievement in the US, usually on a scale from 1 to 4.

C

The Higher Education Achievement Report (HEAR) is an electronic document issued by higher education institutions to students on graduation. It provides a detailed record of a student's academic and extra-curricular achievements to supplement the traditional degree classification. The document contains information:

1 identifying the holder of the qualification;
2 identifying the qualification;
3 on the level of qualification;
4 on the contents and results gained;
5 on the function of the qualification.

D

You are strongly recommended not to bring bags with you to examinations. If you do, you will not be permitted to bring them into the exam room. Also you must not leave bags outside exam rooms where they may cause any kind of obstruction.

There is some limited and mostly unsecured space in the vicinity of exam rooms where if you have to you may leave bags, AT YOUR OWN RISK.

E

On both Open Days, our department sessions will take place at 10 a.m., 12.30 p.m. and 3 p.m. Each session will last around 90 minutes and you can book up to three sessions per day. You must book in advance to secure your place. Our booking system is now open. We already have some sessions full! Don't miss out on your chance to attend one of our departmental talks. Book your place today. If you would like to be added to a waiting list for a fully booked session please contact us at … .

Follow-up

12 Draw up a code of behaviour for your students. You may refer to Texts A and D and online sources.

13 Search online for an English-language description of an academic course which matches your teaching or research interests. Share the results with the class.

Lesson 2 Virtual learning environments

Lead-in

1 Search online for definitions of a 'virtual learning environment'. Look through the search results and choose the best one.

Reading focus

2 Read the title and introduction to an article. Underline the key words that will help you understand the main topic. What do you think the article is about?

Open source e-learning: In the Moodle

Open-source software (OSS) has made a huge impact on the software market. One such product could be about to revolutionise e-learning.

To quote a well-worn adage: if it looks too good to be true, it probably is. There are some exceptions though, and the free-to-download course-management software, Moodle, that also allows users to build e-learning courses and communities, could be one of them.

In the learning sector, Moodle, developed in Australia by the educator and computer scientist Martin Dougiamas, is probably the most high-profile piece of free open-source software (OSS). In simple terms, OSS is software that is developed through public collaboration because anyone can have access to the source code and therefore modify or extend it to suit [1]**their** needs.

3 Answer the questions.

1 Do we have any evidence that the author is impressed with the potential of Moodle?
2 Which specific expressions prove this?

4 Skim read the whole article in two minutes. What is its tone?

- impartial
- critical
- complimentary

5 Read the article again and follow these instructions.

1 How does each heading prepare the reader for what comes next?
2 Identify one sentence that best describes the main idea of each section.

Pedigree

Ray Lawrence, managing director of Telford-based HowToMoodle, which provides training, consultancy and development services to help users get the most from the software, says the 'free' tag may be what attracts people initially, but it is the product's 'pedigree' that is also fuelling its take-up.

'Moodle was developed for educators, not just people with software skills,' he says. 'People in learning and development quickly see that it works.' Those who want to find out more about the pedagogical principles behind the software can do so at www.moodle.org. Partner companies such as HowToMoodle give the 'top slice' of their revenue from Moodle projects back into the software's development. 'It's a virtuous circle and it is what keeps Moodle alive and sustainable,' explains Lawrence. 'It's also what sets it apart from some other open-source software because it means it has a steady flow of income.' Lawrence adds that while it is easy to get carried away with the idea that Moodle is free, part of his company's role is to ensure the software is right for [2]**their** requirements.

Similarly, while Moodle makes it easy to upload content, it is also important to structure the learning activities so they are appropriate for the learner. 'The platform can support communication and reduce administration,' says Dick Moore, director of technology at Ufi and a trustee for The Associaton for Learning Technology. 'But the most critical factor is the quality of the content and course design – that's the differentiator.' Moore adds that to get the most out of it, it is also necessary to have staff who understand the platform at a technical level.

Distance learning

Among HowToMoodle's clients is the Chartered Institute of Housing (CIH), which wanted to run distance-learning courses on an e-learning platform and develop its own e-learning material, as well as drive down costs.

CIH believed an open-source solution would suit their needs, and discovered Moodle. It has since built a Masters degree-level e-learning course to be launched this autumn. It is also looking at how Moodle could be used in other ways, such as using [3]**its** e-portfolio space for members to provide evidence of their competence for chartered status. 'Our aim is to raise the bar on assessment criteria through the use of Moodle,' says Mary James, IT manager at CIH. 'We're investigating how using electronic methods of learning can raise standards of learning compared to classroom environments.' Currently, Moodle has around 40,000 registered sites worldwide, many of [4]**them** private-sector companies. Lawrence says Moodle has given e-learning a welcome shot in the arm. 'A lot of organisations tried e-learning and went through the mill,' he says. 'This time, they want to get it right.' And what better way to dip their toe back in the water than via a piece of free software?

Case study: Customer 1st International

Customer 1st International in Wiltshire produces learning materials and resources to help businesses improve their standards of customer service. It needed a learning-management system for overseas and UK clients, as well as a tutor-led interactive programme that could accommodate learning logs, action plans and assessments. It was aware of Moodle and worked with HowToMoodle to create an online version of the *Best Practice Guide for Customer Service Professionals*. HowToMoodle built the course and provided training so Customer 1st could maintain the course and site after the handover. [5]**It** is now being sold to major blue-chip companies in the UK and abroad. 'Moodle delivered exactly what we wanted,' says Customer 1st managing director Stephanie Edwards. 'It means we have raised the game and can talk about customer service at a higher level.'

6 Scan the article and match the people mentioned in the text (1–5) with their role in regard to Moodle (a–e).

1 Mary James
2 Stephanie Edwards
3 Martin Dougiamas
4 Ray Lawrence
5 Dick Moore

a manages a Moodle consultancy
b created the most well-known OSS
c uses the platform to prove the advantages of e-learning over traditional face-to-face methods
d points out the features that distinguish Moodle from other platforms
e runs the business that uses Moodle to deliver a very specific course for their customers

7 Read the text again and make a list of all the benefits of Moodle. Add to the list if you know of any others.

8 Look at words 1–5 in bold in the article. What do they refer to?

Vocabulary focus

9 As an educational platform, Moodle contains a great deal of specific teaching/learning vocabulary. Read the text on page 31 and create two spidergrams to summarise what students and teachers do differently in Moodle compared to face-to-face teaching/learning, e.g. *students self-enrol*.

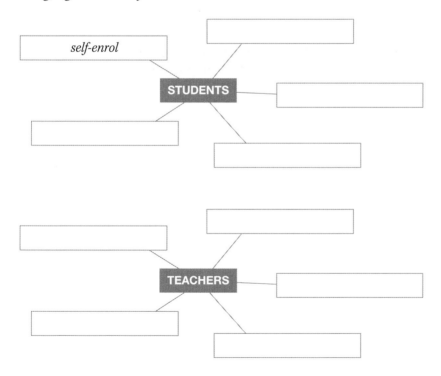

Inside Moodle

- Moodle's basic structure is organised around courses. These are basically pages or areas within Moodle where teachers can present their learning resources and activities to students. They can have different layouts, but they usually include a number of central sections where materials are displayed and have side blocks offering extra features or information.

- Courses can contain content for a year's studies, a single session or any other variants (depending on the teacher or establishment). They can be used by one teacher or shared by a group of teachers.

- How students enrol on courses depends on the establishment; for example they can self-enrol, be enrolled manually by their teacher or automatically by the admin.

- An Activity in Moodle is a feature where students learn by interacting with each other or with their teacher. They might, for instance, contribute in a forum, upload an assignment, answer questions in a quiz or collaborate together in a wiki. Activities can be graded.

- A Resource in Moodle is an item that a teacher can add to a Moodle course to support learning, such as a file, a video or link to a website. A resource differs from an activity in that it is static (i.e. the student can merely look at or read it, rather than participate).

- A course in Moodle is an area where a teacher will add resources and activities for their students to complete. It might be a simple page with downloadable documents or it might be a complex set of activities where learning progresses through interaction. Progress can be tracked in a number of ways.

Follow-up

10 Look on the internet for articles describing possible disadvantages of platforms like Moodle. Write them down and compare your lists in class.

Lesson 3 University research

Lead-in

1 Work in pairs and answer the questions.

1 Does your chair, department or faculty have a website focusing on the academic work done by its members? If yes, what does it contain?
2 Have you visited such websites of other universities? If yes, why?

Reading focus 1

2 Read the text below and say what its function is in a university prospectus.

Whitborn University is one of the leading research universities, renowned for its teaching, research achievements, and social and economic contributions. It has 14 discipline-specific faculties as well as four research institutes, with over 800 faculty members working for 25 academic departments. The University has been host to some of the world's most distinguished scientists, including recipients of the Nobel Prize for Economics. The researchers who supervise and mentor our graduate students are among the world's finest and work at the forefront of international scholarship.

At Whitborn we have identified a core group of research themes that cut across departmental and faculty boundaries. Recognising the multidisciplinary approach to scientific advancement, Whitborn has created four institutes where faculty members, visiting scholars, post-doctoral fellows, graduate and undergraduate students collaborate in exploring four research areas: Life Sciences, Engineering and Applied Sciences, Arts and Humanities, and Social Sciences. This structure allows the examination of emerging trends, and enables the University to respond rapidly to the world's evolving scientific landscape.

3 What information would you expect to find in a text about the research institutes mentioned above?

4 Look through the text *Research Areas* in Activity 5 quickly. Were your predictions correct?

5 Match these topics to the sections in the prospectus.

a research projects aimed at environmental issues
b a search for ways to improve the life of specific groups of people
c development of instruments for research
d a combination of traditional and modern research methodology
e a list of various academic fields
f the connection between research and policy-making

Research Areas

1 Life Sciences

Researchers in the Institute of Life Sciences are tackling the greatest scientific questions we currently face as a society. Be it a micro-biology lab or a field station in the Antarctic, our experimentalists work together with theorists to address complex issues that may affect the lives of people throughout the world – from climate change to influenza outbreaks, from GM food to nuclear power. Expertise and state-of-the-art technology combine to allow multidisciplinary research, teaching and postgraduate training to flourish.

2 Engineering and Applied Sciences

Beyond expanding fundamental human understanding of such areas as chemistry, physics, geology, nanotechnology, and others, research in the Institute of Engineering and Applied Sciences is focused on the application of engineering principles and techniques to find solutions to a broad range of problems including water management, application of computer science in economics, creation of computational tools which can be used both in science and engineering. The researchers that comprise the engineering community are exclusively dedicated to the development of ideas, processes, materials and devices that will improve the lives of people throughout the world.

3 Arts and Humanities

The Institute of Arts and Humanities seeks to promote the study of the cultural history of humankind through the combined efforts of historians, archaeologists, philosophers, art and literary critics and linguists. It places a strong emphasis on traditional humanities, scholarship and practice-led research. Alongside this, some of the projects underway are grounded in new social technologies, in particular, the internet and social software, which advance the interdisciplinary agenda and expand the boundaries of understanding the human condition.

4 Social Sciences

Our Institute for Social Science Research promotes projects encompassing the skills and perspectives needed to solve complex social problems. In addition to engaging with the big issues facing national and global societies, the Institute undertakes high-quality independent research that will assist in furthering social and economic development of disadvantaged local communities. Research in this field attracts increasing numbers of students seeking to develop experience and expertise in political and economic analysis. By taking a critical look at reasons underlying political, social and economic decisions they will be fully prepared to inform public policy effectively.

6 Answer the following questions about the Whitborn University online prospectus.

1 Which characteristic is common to all the research areas described?
2 Which groups of people (researchers, etc.) are mentioned in the text?
3 What specific places where research is carried out are mentioned in the text?
4 What is the role of practice in some of the studies described?
5 What, according to the text, helps the University to identify and study the newest and most urgent problems?

Vocabulary focus

7 Scan the extract from the prospectus in Activity 2 and underline the phrases that include an evaluation of the university and its work, rather than expressing facts. Why do you think they are used here?

8 Look at these sentences from the prospectus in Activities 2 and 5, and identify the function of the phrases in bold.

1 It has 14 discipline-specific faculties **as well as** four cross-disciplinary research institutes ...
2 ... The University has been host to some of the world's most distinguished scientists, **including** recipients of the Nobel Prize ...
3 ... computational tools which can be used **both** in science **and** engineering
4 ... some of the projects underway are grounded in new social technologies, **in particular,** the internet and social software, ...
5 **In addition to** engaging with the big issues facing national and global societies, the Institute...

9 Complete the sentences with the phrases in bold from Activity 8.

1 _____ taking 'core' courses, which are essentially taught in the first two years of study, and the final-year project, students may choose from optional units.
2 The project will involve researchers from each of the ten countries, _____ the US.
3 Technology transfer in its broadest sense includes information, demonstration and the transfer of knowledge and skills _____ licensing agreements.
4 Efforts will also be made to increase participation by women researchers, _____ by designing the actions in a way that allows researchers to achieve an appropriate work–life balance and by facilitating resuming a research career after a break.
5 The study describes _____ British _____ American history teacher training systems.

10 Look at the prospectus in Activities 2 and 5 again.

1 Find and underline the following words in the text:
a	field	**f**	furthering
b	develop	**g**	examination
c	scholarship	**h**	allow
d	address	**i**	perspectives
e	issues	**j**	tools

2 Now scan the text again to find words with a similar meaning to a–j. Note that the part of speech may be different, e.g. *develop – evolving*.

11 Match the words (1–8) with the meaning the word has in the prospectus.

1 inform
    a to tell someone about particular facts
    b to influence someone's attitude or opinion

2 condition
    a the physical situation that someone or something is in and affected by
    b an arrangement that must exist before something else can happen
    c the particular state that something or someone is in

3 scholarship
    a an amount of money given by a school, college, university or other organisation to pay for the studies of a person
    b serious, detailed study

4 focus
    a to try to look directly at an object so that you can see it more clearly
    b to move a device on the lens of a camera or microscope so that you can see a clear picture
    c the main or central point of something, especially of attention or interest

5 discipline
    a training which produces obedience (= willingness to obey) or self-control
    b ability to control yourself or other people
    c a particular area of study, especially a subject studied at a university
    d to teach someone to behave in a controlled way

6 critical
    a saying that someone or something is bad or wrong
    b of the greatest importance to the way things might happen in the future
    c extremely serious or dangerous
    d giving opinions or judgments on books, plays, films, etc.

7 fellow
    a someone who has the same job or interests as you
    b a member of a group of teachers of high rank at a college or university
    c a member of an official organisation for a particular subject or job

8 advance
    a to go, or move forward
    b to develop or improve something
    c the forward movement of something
    d development or improvement

Reading focus 2

12 You are going to read about the results of a survey. Before reading, study the diagrams. Predict what the survey is about.

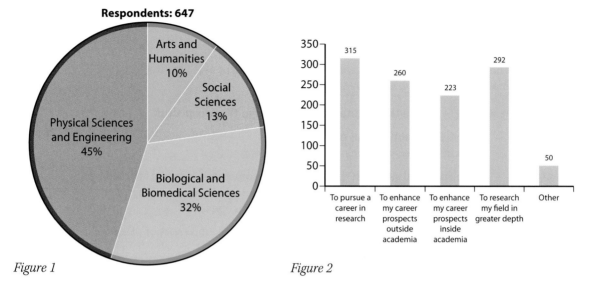

Figure 1   Figure 2

13 Read about the survey and answer the questions.

1 Were your predictions correct?
2 Can you think of a title for the text?
3 What is the purpose of the text?

The UK GRAD Programme works with employers, universities, researchers and other stakeholders to embed personal and professional development for postgraduate researchers. We conducted this survey to better understand postgraduate researchers' motivations for undertaking a PhD and to gain an insight into their career expectations. We hope that this data may be useful to recruiters and potential recruiters targeting the PhD sector and in developing resource plans. Additionally, we hope that the data may be useful to anyone interested in the career motivations and expectations of UK doctoral researchers.

In order to gain a better understanding of the views of the PhD researchers themselves, we have conducted a survey that asks about their career expectations. This research was conducted during October 2005, via an online survey, which was distributed through the UK GRAD Hub and the National Postgraduate Committee networks.

It was apparent from those surveyed that their reasons for undertaking a PhD are complex, diverse and wide-ranging. We asked respondents to indicate their core reasons for undertaking a PhD (see Figure 2). Respondents could select more than one reason. The data shows that 34% of respondents were undertaking a PhD to enhance their career prospects **inside** academia and that 49% wanted to pursue a career in research. 45% of respondents indicated that the chance to research their field in greater depth was a core reason for further study. It is interesting that 40% considered that undertaking a PhD would enhance their career prospects **outside** the academic sphere.

The themes emerging from the survey are as follows.

Motivations

There are a wide variety and breadth of reasons why individuals undertake a PhD. The complex interplay of motivations and reasons that underpin career choice thus far is a key factor in understanding how best to support our research students in thinking about careers.

Career expectations

Although the survey group seem to have considered the benefits to their career of undertaking a PhD, they are not clear about what that career actually looks like or about the career opportunities available to them.

Bridging the knowledge gap

The responses to the survey highlight that there is still some distance to travel before researchers feel aware of the information and the opportunities available to them – both in terms of future career options and their approach to career choices and decision making.

To best support our researchers, we need to be able to understand their career intentions in the longer term. Researchers need information, advice and guidance to help them think about both academic and non-academic career opportunities. They also need to be able to understand their own preferences about style of workplace, management, culture, etc. and those of potential employers, in order to make decisions based on values and motivations.

14 Study the information in Activity 12 and answer the following questions.

1 Judging by the breakdown of the respondents by subject, in which research areas is more progress likely to be made?
2 How many PhD students took part in the survey? What is the total number of responses in Figure 2? Why is there a difference between the numbers?
3 To which group of responses in Figure 2 do all of the following reasons belong?
   • 'To further myself intellectually'
   • 'To put off thinking about a career'
   • 'To stand out from the crowd'

Follow-up

15 Search online for descriptions of research programmes at your faculty/university (or any other university in your country with an English website) and any university abroad. Then compare the texts.

1 Do the texts contain similar information (or emphasise the same points)?
2 What other differences (or similarities) did you find?

16 Work in pairs or small groups to compare your findings. Then report to the class.

Unit 3 Academic publications

By the end of this unit you will be able to

⇒ identify the reader, type and purpose of academic texts

⇒ examine features of academic texts

⇒ understand similarities and differences between texts

⇒ understand relations between parts of a text

⇒ understand the structure of abstracts and popular science articles

Lesson 1 Publishing matters

Lead-in

1 Work in pairs and answer the questions.

1 How do you usually search for publications you need to read?
2 What types of published materials do you find most helpful in your teaching or research?

Reading focus

2 Are you familiar with these international magazines and journals? What is their target readership?

- *Scientific American*
- *The Economist*
- *Teaching Sociology*

- *Cosmopolitan*
- *Journal of Conflict Resolution*
- *Business & Management Review*

3 The texts below are all intended for different categories of reader. Read them quickly and identify their target readership. What helps you to decide?

A

The **Oxford Review of Education** is a well established journal with an extensive international readership. It is committed to deploying the resources of a wide range of academic disciplines in the service of educational scholarship, and the editors welcome articles reporting significant new research as well as contributions of a more analytic or reflective nature. The membership of the editorial board reflects these emphases, which have remained characteristic of the **Review** since its foundation. The **Review** seeks to preserve the highest standards of professional scholarship in education, while also seeking to publish articles which will be of interest and utility to a wider public, including policy makers. Papers submitted to the **Oxford Review of Education** are read by two referees whose comments guide the Editors towards their final decision. The editorial board meets twice a year and takes responsibility for the general development of the Journal.

Peer Review Policy

All research articles in this journal have undergone rigorous peer review, based on initial editor screening and from at least two anonymous referees.

B

Effect of low light and high noise on behavioural activity, physiological indicators of stress and production in laying hens

O'Connor EA, Parker MO, Davey EL, Grist H, Owen RC, Szladovits B, Demmers TG, Wathes CM, Abeyesinghe SM.

Abstract

1. Commercial laying hens are commonly housed in noisy and dim environments, yet relatively little is known about whether these conditions, particularly in combination, have any effect on welfare or egg production.

2. The study was designed to investigate whether chronic exposure to continuous noise (60 dB(A) vs. 80 dB(A)) and/or light intensity (150 lux vs. 5 lux) during the critical period of coming into lay (16–24 weeks of age) influenced behaviour, physiological stress (heterophil to lymphocyte ratio) and production (number and weight of eggs laid) in laying hens.

3. Hens in the low light pens were less active and preened and dust-bathed more than those housed in 150 lux; hens in the high noise pens rested more frequently than those in quieter pens.

4. There was no evidence that chronic exposure to low light or high noise caused appreciable physiological stress but egg production was affected by these conditions. Hens kept in pens with low light or high noise laid fewer eggs per day than those kept in high light or low noise pens.

5. These results show that low light intensity and continual high background noise have a detrimental effect on egg production in the early laying phase, as well as influencing the time allocated to different behaviours. However, there was no strong evidence for a physiological stress response to either of these conditions or their combination.

C

The Editor who has approached you may not know your work intimately, and may only be aware of your work in a broader context. Only accept an invitation if the article is within your area of expertise.

Depending upon the journal, you will be asked to evaluate the article on a number of criteria. Some journals provide detailed guidance others do not, but normally you would be expected to evaluate the article according to the following: *originality*, *structure*, *previous research*, *ethical issues*.

Originality

Is the article sufficiently novel and interesting to warrant publication? Does it add to the canon of knowledge? Does the article adhere to the journal's standards? Is the research question an important one? In order to determine its originality and appropriateness for the journal, it might be helpful to think of the research in terms of what percentile it is in. Is it in the top 25% of papers in this field? You might wish to do a quick literature search using tools such as Scopus to see if there are any reviews of the area.

D

A journal with an interdisciplinary approach to problems and research in the field of interaction between ICT and humans, *Computer Monthly* is a publishing platform for theoretical and methodological papers in computer science and related disciplines. *CM* accepts articles, whose research scale, scope and novelty may lead to new perspectives and, eventually, major breakthroughs across the spectrum of disciplines.

Humans in the Computer World

CM strives to highlight the set of complex relationships between human beings and ICT, putting special emphasis on analysing the cognitive components, organisational and societal factors of ICT. Theoretical articles should seek to tackle a range of learning or performance-related issues whereas empirical papers are supposed to cover more hands-on studies, from laboratory experiments to surveys. Methodological articles submitted to the journal should deal specifically with study of research methods.

User Interfaces

One of the disciplines closely related to ICT, ubiquitous, and, therefore, appealing to the journal's readership is system design. *CM* welcomes contributions from scientists and scholars reporting on their research efforts in creating novel interfaces, analysing the existing models and discussing design techniques. Theoretical papers on this topic should cover the underlying principles of user interfaces, their classification guidelines and their impact on ICT–human interaction. Empirical articles may deal with issues ranging from the process of new interface development to laboratory tests on its efficiency

4 Answer the questions below about Texts A–D.

1 Which of the texts contains information given in brackets? Why are they used?
2 Which information is given in **bold**? Why?
3 What is written in *italics* in the texts?
4 Explain the logic behind the sections in each text.

5 Read Texts A and C and find pronouns which are used as subjects.

1 What do they refer to?
2 Is the style of texts the same or different? Why?

6 An abstract usually has a standard structure. Put the elements of an abstract below in order. Does the abstract in Text B have all these elements?

a Findings
b Reason for writing
c Conclusions
d Methodology/Process
e Problem

7 Now read the abstract below (E) and answer the questions.

1 Does this abstract have the same structure as the abstract in Text B? Does it contain all the elements listed in Activity 6?

2 What are the major differences between the two abstracts (and the articles they present)?

3 Which types of article mentioned in Text D would they belong to?

E

Professional identity development: a review of the higher education literature

Franziska Trede, Rob Macklin & Donna Bridges

This study examined the extant higher education literature on the development of professional identities. Through a systematic review approach 20 articles were identified that discussed in some way professional identity development in higher education journals. These articles drew on varied theories, pedagogies and learning strategies; however, most did not make a strong connection to professional identities. Further research is needed to better understand the tensions between personal and professional values, structural and power influences, discipline versus generic education, and the impact of workplace learning on professional identities.

8 Text E contains some words or expressions that you may not know. Without consulting a dictionary, try to guess what the following words mean. What helps you decide?

> extant   drew on   generic

9 An abstract helps readers find materials relevant to their research. What other parts of a journal article can you consult to decide if you need to read all of it?

Vocabulary focus

> **Tip:**
> Noun + noun combinations (e.g. *computer systems*) are often used in academic texts, as they allow authors to express information in a concise way.

10 Work in pairs and follow the instructions.

1 Individually, scan the texts in this lesson for three minutes to find as many noun + noun combinations as possible. Write them down.

2 Compare your list with your partner's. Combine your lists.

3 Work with other pairs and take turns to show your combined lists. Whose list is longer? Share your results with the class.

11 Work in pairs. Put the noun + noun combinations from Activity 10 in groups. Decide on your criteria for grouping. Compare your results with other pairs.

12 Which text in this lesson contains the least number of noun + noun combinations, and which contains the most? Why do you think that is?

13 The word *novel* can refer to a long story about imaginary characters and events. What is the meaning of *novel* in Texts C and D?

> **Tip:**
> Many words (e.g. *subject, review, novel*) can have more than one meaning, depending on whether they are used as a noun, a verb or an adjective.

14 Read the definitions and try to guess words 1–5.

1 _____
    a to produce or provide something official (verb)
    b a subject or problem which people are thinking and talking about (noun)
    c a single copy of a newspaper, magazine or journal (noun)
    d a set of articles in a magazine or journal published at the same time (noun)

2 _____
    a to consider something in order to make changes to it, give an opinion on it (verb)
    b the process of carefully examining a situation or somebody's work to find out whether changes or improvements need to be made (noun)
    c a report in a newspaper, magazine, or programme that gives an opinion about a new book, film, etc. (noun)
    d a newspaper, magazine or journal that has articles on films, books, travel, research, etc. (noun)

3 _____
    a existing as an idea, feeling or quality, not as a material object (adjective)
    b a shortened form of a speech, article, book, etc., giving only the most important facts or ideas (noun)
    c a type of painting which represents the qualities of something, not its outer appearance (adjective)

4 _____
    a an area of land in the country where crops are grown (noun)
    b an area of activity or interest (noun)
    c place outside an office or laboratory where practical work and research is done (noun)

Follow-up

15 Search online for 2–3 abstracts of articles in your field of study.

1 Compare the abstracts you found with the samples in this lesson.
2 Which of the samples do they most look like?
3 Is there anything missing from the sample abstracts in this lesson?

16 Make lists of key words from the abstracts you found. (If they already contain key terms, add some more to the list.)

17 Work in pairs. Exchange your lists of key words. Read them and guess the topics of your partner's articles and the main contents.

Lesson 2 Popular science articles

Lead-in

1 Do you read popular science articles? Why? On what occasions?

Reading focus 1

2 The reading material below contains eight passages from two popular science articles. Read passages a–h quickly and match them to article titles 1 and 2.

1 Atheists turn to science during times of stress
2 Take a peek inside the brain's filing cabinet

a Gradually, a map emerged showing which neurons each noun and verb activates. The neural activity seems to occur in logical groups. Voxels active for animals such as dogs and fish tend to cluster close to one another, for instance. Other links are less easy to interpret: vehicles and animals are grouped together, perhaps because both are capable of movement.

b Farias speculates that a rationalist outlook would provide similar relief. 'Any kind of belief system helps you structure your perception of reality,' he says. 'It allows you to think of the universe in a particular meaningful way'. The researchers have begun a similar study using scientists who are religious to see how the two belief systems interact in response to stress.

c Our brains are master organisers, able to make sense of the constant stream of visual information we encounter every day. A new map of the brain gives some insight into how it does this.

d A team of psychologists led by Miguel Farias at the University of Oxford asked 52 rowers to fill in a 'belief in science' questionnaire just before taking part in a competitive regatta. They gave the same test – in which participants had to score statements such as 'science is the most valuable part of human culture' – to a similar number of rowers at a training session. The questionnaire also assessed self-reported stress levels and degree of religious belief

e Recent studies have suggested that the brain organises the things we see into categories, such as animals or faces. To determine how this categorisation works, Jack Gallant at the University of California, Berkeley, and colleagues identified the 1,705 most commonly used nouns and verbs in the English language. They then showed video clips of these objects and actions to four people as each lay in an fMRI scanner, and recorded the brain responses. The team divided the fMRI images up into tiny squares, or voxels. When a video clip of an object such as a butterfly was played, the fMRI recorded which voxels – and hence which groups of neurons – were active.

f Farias and colleagues discovered that those about to race were both more stressed, and rated their belief in science 14% higher than those who were simply training. Some caveats: the effect was modest, the team didn't measure whether the rowers' stress levels went down, and the subjects – competitive athletes who follow a rational training regime – are probably already scientifically minded. However, the findings reflect a growing body of psychological evidence that people find comfort in times of threat by moving closer to certain aspects of their world view – conservatives become more conservative, for example, liberals more liberal, religious believers more devout.

43

g It's well known that religious faith can help believers cope with stress and anxiety, by providing them with a sense of meaning and control at times of uncertainty. It now seems that a 'belief' in science and a rationalistic outlook might do the same for the non-religious.

h Gallant says the results suggest that the brain organises visual information by its relationship to other information. Each neuron appears to act as a 'filter' for placing data into multiple categories. The method opens a new door to looking at brain data, says John-Dylan Haynes of the Bernstein Center for Computational Neuroscience in Berlin, Germany.

3 Read passages a–h again and match them to these sections of an article. What helps you decide?

1 introduction/general information
2 description of the experiment
3 findings
4 researchers' comments and prospects of future research

4 Work in pairs. Note down the main points of each text from Activity 2 on the following spidergram. Student A: work with Text 1. Student B: work with Text 2.

5 Ask your partner questions based on your spidergram. Check what they remember from your text.

Vocabulary focus 1

6 Research can be divided into three stages: planning, process and analysing results. Read Texts 1–2 again and complete the table with expressions describing these stages.

Example: *gave the same test (process)* ...

Planning	Process	Results

Reading focus 2

7 Skim the article below and summarise it in one or two sentences.

Research agenda set for curbing US gun violence

Barack Obama asked for a new agenda for research into curbing gun violence, and now he has one.

Just one problem: getting a Congress that rejected his plans for tighter gun laws in the wake of the Newtown massacre to provide the necessary cash.

In January, Obama directed the Centers for Disease Control and Prevention (CDC) to identify pressing questions about reducing deaths and injuries caused by guns. [1]_____ Then Congressional allies of the National Rifle Association slashed the agency's annual budget by $2.6 million – the exact sum it had been spending on gun violence research.

Now an Institute of Medicine panel headed by Alan Leshner, CEO of the American Association for the Advancement of Science, has given the CDC a list of priorities for investigation, ranging from the potential of 'smart guns' that only their registered user can fire, to the effectiveness of childhood education programmes in reducing violence in later life.

[2]_____ Many previous studies have simply looked for correlations between policies across different countries or US states and their rates of gun violence, and so have not been able to demonstrate causation.

'We don't just need more research but more rigorous research,' agrees Garen Wintemute, who heads the Violence Prevention Research Program at the University of California, Davis.

[3]_____ Any addition to the CDC's budget would require Congressional approval, and that will be hard to obtain, given the gun lobby's powerful influence. 'Everything on this list has been controversial all along,' says Wintemute. 'That controversy will remain.'

---

8 Complete the article with sentences a–c. What elements of the text help you to decide?

a The panel also wants future research to be more rigorous, based on controlled trials or before-and-after studies that can show cause and effect for specific interventions.

b The big question, however, is where the money is going to come from.

c That ended a de facto freeze on such research that had been in place since the mid-1990s.

9 The article consists of six parts. For each part, write down the key words expressing its main idea, e.g. paragraph 1: *problem, Congress, gun laws.*

Vocabulary focus 2

10 Read the text again. Find expressions describing the stages of research and add them to the table in Activity 6.

Follow-up

11 Search online for a recent popular science article. Summarise its contents.

12 Work in pairs. Take turns to give the gist of the article to your partner and ask him/her to suggest a title.

Lesson 3 Research reports

Lead-in

1 Work in pairs. Read the following definitions of *research* and *report*. Then, work in pairs and give your own definition of a *research report*. Compare your definition with other pairs and choose the best one. Explain your choice.

> • *research* – a detailed study of a subject, especially in order to discover (new) information or reach a (new) understanding.
>
> • *report* – a description of an event or situation

Reading focus

2 Complete the table with the research report elements.

> Abstract/Synopsis   Appendices   Conclusion   Discussion
> Literature Review (sometimes included in the Introduction)
> References or Bibliography   Results   Title of report

Parts	Sections
Preliminary material	1 _____
	2 Table of Contents (not always required)
	3 _____
Body of report	4 Introduction
	5 _____
	6 Methodology
	7 _____
	8 _____
	9 _____
	10 Recommendations (sometimes included in the Conclusion)
Supplementary material	11 _____
	12 _____

3 Work in pairs and list all the stages involved in preparing a report and what you do at each stage.

4 Read stages a–g of research report preparation suggested by the Adelaide Writing Centre. Put them in order. Then compare your ideas in pairs.

a Draft the supplementary material.
b Analyse the task.
c Do the research.
d Improve your report.
e Draft the body of your report.
f Develop a rough plan.
g Draft the preliminary material.

5 Compare your ideas with the suggested list from the Adelaide Writing Centre. How similar/different are your stages and the ones in Activity 3? Why do you think this might be?

6 Match sections 1–12 from Activity 2 with the information below they should include.

a all the references used in your report or referred to for background information
b any additional material which will add to your report
c concise heading indicating what the report is about
d concise summary of main findings
e list of major sections and headings with page numbers
f other relevant research in this area
g relevance of your results, how it fits with other research in the area
h summary of results/findings
i what needs to be done as a result of your findings
j what you did and how you did it
k what you found
l why and what you researched

7 Read the summary of the following research report. What is the topic of the report?

Executive summary (Summary or abstract)

The aim of this report was to investigate UniLab staff attitudes to personal mobile phone use in staff and team meetings. A staff survey on attitudes towards the use of mobile phones in the staff/team meetings was conducted. The results indicate that the majority of staff find mobile phone use a major issue in staff meetings. The report concludes that personal mobile phones are disruptive and should be turned off in meetings. It is recommended that UniLab develops a company policy banning the use of mobile phones except in exceptional circumstances.

8 Read the whole report. Which of the sections mentioned in Activity 2 are missing or are in a different order?

Introduction

There has been a massive increase in the use of personal mobile phones over the past five years and there is every indication that this will continue. According to Black (2002), by 2008, almost 100% of working people in Australia will carry personal mobile phones. Black describes this phenomenon as 'serious in the extreme, potentially undermining the foundations of communication in our society' (2002). Currently at UniLab, 89% of staff have personal mobile phones.

Recently, a number of staff have complained about the use of personal mobile phones in meetings and asked what the official company policy is. At present there is no official company policy regarding phone use. This report examines the issue of mobile phone usage in staff meetings and small team meetings. It does not seek to examine the use of mobile phones in the workplace at other times, although some concerns were raised.

For the purposes of this report a personal mobile phone is a personally funded phone for private calls as opposed to an employer funded phone that directly relates to carrying out a particular job.

Methods

This research was conducted by questionnaire and investigated UniLab staff members' attitudes to the use of mobile phones in staff/team meetings. A total of 412 questionnaires were distributed with employees' fortnightly pay slips (see Appendix 1). The questionnaire used Likert scales to assess social attitudes (Smith 2002) to mobile phone usage and provided open-ended responses for additional comments. Survey collection boxes were located in every branch for a four week period. No personal information was collected; the survey was voluntary and anonymous.

Results

There was an 85% response rate to the questionnaire. A breakdown of the responses is listed below in Table 1. It can be clearly seen from the results that mobile phones are considered to be disruptive and should be turned off in meetings.

Table 1

Personal mobile phone usage in staff and team meetings is …	strongly agree (%)	agree (%)	disagree (%)	strongly disagree (%)
not a problem	5	7	65	23
an issue	40	45	10	5
disruptive	80	10	7	3
phones should be permissible	6	16	56	22
phones should be turned off	85	10	3	2
allowed in some circumstances	10	52	24	14

The survey also allowed participants to identify any circumstances where mobile phones should be allowed in meetings and also assessed staff attitudes towards receiving personal phone calls in staff meetings in open-ended questions. These results showed that staff thought that in some circumstances (e.g. medical or emergencies), receiving personal phone calls was acceptable, but generally receiving personal phone calls was not necessary.

Discussion/Interpretation of results

It can be seen from the results in Table 1 that personal mobile phone use is considered to a problem. However, it was acknowledged that in some situations it should be permissible: 80% of recipients considered mobile phones to be highly disruptive and there was strong support for phones being turned off in meetings (85%). Only 12% thought that mobile phone usage in staff and team meetings was not a problem, whereas 85% felt it was an issue. The results are consistent throughout the survey. Many of the respondents (62%) felt that in exceptional circumstances mobile phones should be allowed (e.g. medical) but there should be protocols regarding this.

These findings are consistent with other studies. According to Smith (2005), many companies have identified mobile phones as disruptive and have banned the use of mobile phones in meetings. Havir (2004) claims that 29% of staff-meeting time is wasted through unnecessary mobile phone interruptions. This affects time management, productivity and team focus.

Conclusion

The use of mobile phones in staff meetings is clearly disruptive and they should be switched off. Most staff felt it is not necessary to receive personal phone calls in staff meetings except under certain circumstances, but permission should first be sought from the team leader, manager or chair.

Recommendations

It is recommended that UniLab develops an official policy regarding the use of mobile phones in staff meetings. The policy should recommend:
• mobile phones are banned in staff meetings
• mobiles phone may be used in exceptional circumstances but only with the permission of the appropriate manager or chair
Finally, the policy needs to apply to all staff in the company.

9 Read the report again and decide if the following statements are true or false. Correct the false ones.

1 The goal of this report was to study company staff attitudes to personal mobile phone use in meetings.
2 It is recommended that the company develops a policy completely banning the use of mobile phones.
3 There was an immense increase in the use of mobile phones seven years ago.
4 This research was conducted using a questionnaire.
5 Personal information of respondents was collected to make the survey more reliable.
6 Only 6% of respondents strongly agree that mobile phones should be allowed in meetings.

10 Read conclusions A–C to different research reports. Fill in the gaps with the words below.

alternative analysis hypothesis opportunities
problem programmes similar standards

A

The stomach contents of the red eft, red-backed salamander, and dusky salamander living in the same area were identified. An **1**_____ of the food eaten shows that the feeding habits of the red eft and the red-backed salamander were different. These two salamanders showed 'niche segregation'. These two salamanders ate **2**_____ food when living in different areas but fed on different food when the two species lived in the same area. Our **3**_____ was valid.

B

The **4**_____ of teen gang violence can be eliminated. It will, however, take time, money, and a combined effort on the part of many people. Organised, free, after-school programmes such as: sports teams and games; art, music, and drama activities; internships in local area businesses and professional organisations; and interesting volunteer activities in the community would help engage teens in worthwhile pursuits outside of school hours. More job **5**_____ for teens, especially those funded by state and local programmes, would offer income for teens as well as productive work for the community. Outreach to families through schools, community organisations, and places of worship would help promote inter-generational activities that could improve family closeness, helping teens to work on their problems at the family level, instead of taking them to the streets. If these **6**_____ can be implemented, we will surely see a decrease in teen gang activity and safer streets and neighbourhoods for us all.

C

Two **7**_____ designs for an emission-free fuel cell powered car have been presented: Car A, a luxury sedan which runs on hydrogen, and Car B, a medium-sized family hatch which uses hydrogen and oxygen. Each car features recyclable materials and conforms to Australian design **8**_____ in terms of performance and safety features. However, Car B is recommended as it was found to be more economical in terms of both manufacturing and running costs.

11 Work in pairs. Read conclusions A–C again and answer the questions.

1 What fields of research do these reports refer to?
2 Think of titles for these reports.

Vocabulary focus

12 Match nouns 1–7 from the research report in Activity 8 to their definitions.

1 phenomenon
2 response
3 findings
4 questionnaire
5 purpose
6 survey
7 method

a a set of questions people are asked to gather information or find out their opinions
b a way of doing something, often one that involves a system or plan
c why you do something or why something exists
d a written list of questions that people are asked so that information can be collected
e something that exists or happens, usually something unusual
f something said or done as a reaction to something that has been said or done
g information that has been discovered

13 Complete the sentences with the nouns from Activity 12.

1 Visitors to the country have been asked to fill in a detailed _____.
2 A recent _____ revealed that 58% of people did not know where their heart is.
3 The report's _____ on the decrease in violent crime support the police chief's claims.
4 The new teaching _____ encourages children to think for themselves.
5 The _____ of the research is to try and find out more about the causes of the disease.
6 Her proposals met with an enthusiastic _____.

14 Match the words from the report (1–7) with words with a similar meaning (a–g).

1 examine   **a** permit
2 recommend   **b** influence
3 assess   **c** evaluate
4 allow   **d** think
5 consider   **e** investigate
6 acknowledge   **f** admit
7 affect   **g** advise

Follow-up

15 Search online for tips and recommendations on writing a research report. Do you agree with them? Can you add more? Choose the best ones and share them with the class.

Unit 4 International cooperation

By the end of this unit you will be able to

➡ consolidate the skills developed in the Reading module

➡ recognise a writer's intention and attitude

➡ identify the functions of different types of text

➡ select and present information from different texts in the form of a table

➡ develop awareness of linguistic features of different genre texts on international cooperation

➡ understand relations between parts of a text describing grant programmes

Lesson 1 International cooperation programmes

Lead-in

1 **Work in pairs and answer the questions below.**

1 Have you ever worked on an international project? (When? Who with? What was the project?)

2 What other forms of international academic cooperation do you know?

Reading focus 1

2 **Read Text A about a European programme of international cooperation.**

1 Divide it into four paragraphs.

2 Say what helped you do it.

A

The Tempus programme, which is the longest-standing EU programme in the educational sector and which has a strong focus on cooperation between higher education institutions, has entered a new phase running from 2007 to 2013. Since its inception in 1990, university cooperation under the Tempus programme has contributed successfully to institution building in higher education in the Partner Countries and to sustainable university partnerships, as well as to enhancing mutual understanding between the academic worlds of the European Union and the Partner Countries. Particularly in the Partner Countries, higher education institutions are currently facing major challenges linked to dramatic demographic changes (number of people potentially having access to higher education, age structure, migration flows), increasing global competition, leading to a considerable shift in the distribution of the economic power at world level, changes in science and technology but notably the growing importance of organisational and societal innovation rather than purely technological innovation and, last but not least, challenges of societies in transition (social cohesion, human rights, etc.). Higher education institutions are therefore key players in the successful transition to a knowledge-based economy and society and they provide the training for a new generation of leaders. They are the pools of expertise and centres for the development of human resources. Higher education institutions are also important factors in growth and competitiveness, and play a crucial role in the reform agenda of both EU Member States and the Tempus Partner Countries. The overall aim of Tempus is to contribute to the creation of an area of cooperation in the field of higher education between the European Union and the Tempus Partner Countries. The specific objectives of Tempus are as follows: to promote the reform and modernisation of higher education in the Partner Countries; to enhance the quality and relevance of higher education to the world of work and society in the Partner Countries; to increase the capacity of higher education institutions in the Partner Countries and the EU, in particular their capacity to cooperate internationally and to continually modernise; to assist them in opening up to the world of work and the society at large; to foster the reciprocal development of human resources; and to enhance mutual understanding between the peoples and cultures of the EU and the Partner Countries.

3 Work in pairs. Compare your paragraphing and suggest a heading for each paragraph. Report back to the class.

4 Is the style of the text formal or informal? What language features show it?

5 In Text A find:

1 all the instances where information is presented in a slightly biased way
2 sentences where numbering or bullet points could be used to make the text read more clearly
3 a description of the core mission of HE institutions

Vocabulary focus

6 Search Text A for different ways of emphasising or adding to a point. Write the words or phrases down.

7 Fill the gaps in the following sentences with the words you found in Activity 6.

1 In a number of European states, however, _____ England and Holland, the freedom with which researchers could defend the Copernican system stands in surprising contrast with the criticism faced by Galileo.
2 According to the research, the setting up of a stock exchange was indispensable for enhancing the flow of capital and for the creation of a market in securities, _____ for protecting the interests of venture capitalists.
3 The applications referred to in Section A are _____: a) an application for the renewal of a licence; b) an application for a new licence; c) an application for a permanent transfer of a licence.
4 The course offers comprehensive training in communication theory, _____ in the academic context.

Reading focus 2

8 Read Text B quickly and say: a) what it focuses on; b) what features of the text help you answer.

B

The 'People' Specific Programme acknowledges that one of the main competitive edges in science and technology is the quantity and quality of its human resources. To support the further development and consolidation of the European Research Area, this Specific Programme's overall strategic objective is to make Europe more attractive for the best researchers.

The Specific Programme aims to strengthen, quantitatively and qualitatively, the human potential in research and technology in Europe, by stimulating people to enter into the profession of researcher, encouraging European researchers to stay in Europe, and attracting to Europe researchers from the entire world, making Europe more attractive to the best researchers. Building on the experiences with the 'Marie Curie' actions under previous Framework Programmes, this will be done by putting into place a coherent set of 'Marie Curie' actions, particularly taking into account the European added value in terms of their structuring effect on the European Research Area. These actions address researchers at all stages of their careers, in the public and private sectors, from initial research training, specifically intended for young people, to lifelong learning and career development. Efforts will also be made to increase participation by women researchers, by encouraging equal opportunities in all 'Marie Curie Actions', by designing the actions to ensure that researchers can achieve an appropriate work/life balance and by facilitating resuming a research career after a break.

9 Read Texts A and B again and complete the table below.

Information	Text A	Text B
Background of the programme		
Territory		
Participants		
General aim		
Causes of existing problems		—

10 Read the second sentence in Text B. How do the two parts of the sentence relate to each other?

a cause and effect
b repeating the same idea
c the end and means to the end
d topic and illustration

To support the further development and consolidation of the European Research Area,

this Specific Programme's overall strategic objective is to make Europe more attractive for the best researchers.

11 Read Text B again.

1 Identify two sentences which express an aim.
2 In each sentence, identify the three means of achieving the aim.
3 What language structures are used to perform the functions?

12 Read the end of Text B and say what the phrases a) *an appropriate work/life balance* and b) *resuming a career after a break* imply in this context.

Follow-up

13 On the internet, find information about an international project/initiative/programme that you might be interested in. Make notes about it in the form of a table (as in Activity 9 but you can add more parts to it). Report to the group.

Lesson 2 Grants

Lead-in

1 Which of the following activities may be supported by a grant of some kind?

- a research project
- a visit to a university abroad to meet fellow researchers
- writing a textbook in your subject
- organising an international seminar

2 Have you ever applied for a grant for any of these activities? Were you successful or not? Why?

Reading focus 1

3 Match these typical functions of texts about grants and international cooperation (1–5) with extracts A–D below. (There is one extra function on the list that you do not need.)

1 informing	4 warning
2 inviting	5 giving instructions
3 telling a success story	

A

Are you an experienced researcher looking for a postdoctoral fellowship?
Submit your grant application for the IEF scheme and gain the opportunity to acquire new research skills or to work in other sectors.

B

- Fill out the Software Grant application Form – we encourage you to develop this with a project team and recommend that you keep a copy for your records.

- Sign the Programme Authorisation Form. The Grant Application <u>must</u> be endorsed by both the Lead Institute Director/Principal as well as Director/Principal of any participating organisation.

- Submit the Application and Authorisation forms to: *Innovative Teachers Programme Manager*.

C

Peter Tóth is a Marie Curie IEF fellow. Through his BIOBROOM project, he has developed a biological control method against 'broomrapes', parasitic weeds that would be eliminated by flies, making the use of herbicides unnecessary.

D

Period 2 will be open from 15 September to 31 October. Grant recipients will be **notified** by 1 December and will be **awarded** grants for two years, beginning on 1 January and ending 31 December. Projects may **commence** in the spring term.

Grant recipients will be eligible to apply for subsequent grants after the **initial** two year period.

4 What contents and language features of Texts A–D helped you decide on their functions?

5 In Text D, what words can be used instead of the words in bold?

Reading focus 2

6 Work as quickly as possible. Scan Text E to find answers to the following questions.

1 How many sections are there in the Table of Contents?
2 Which parts of the proposal have no page limit?
3 What happens if some parts of the proposal are longer than the instruction requires?
4 Which section mentions the need for the proposed project to be up to date?
5 What is/are the guiding document(s) for evaluation criteria?

E

> To draft PART B of proposals, applicants should take into account the following structure. If required for an adequate description of their project, applicants can add further subheadings. Applicants must ensure that sections B1, B2 (except the CV), B3 and B4 do not exceed the given page limits. Experts will be instructed to disregard any excess pages.

Table of Contents

B1 SCIENTIFIC AND TECHNOLOGICAL QUALITY (MAXIMUM 7 PAGES)
  B1.1 Research and technological quality, including any interdisciplinary and multidisciplinary aspects of the proposal
  B1.2 Appropriateness of research methodology and approach
  B1.3 Originality and innovative nature of the project, and relationship to the 'state of the art' of research in the field
  B1.4 Timeliness and relevance of the project

B2 QUALITY OF THE RESEARCHER (SECTIONS B2.1–B2.4: MAXIMUM 5 PAGES)
  B2.1 Research career potential
  B2.2 Research and technological quality of previous research*
  B2.3 Independent thinking and leadership qualities
  B2.4 Match between the fellow's profile and project
  B2.5 Curriculum Vitae – NO PAGE LIMIT

B3 IMPLEMENTATION (MAXIMUM 4 PAGES)
  B3.1 Quality of host organisation, including adequacy of infrastructures/facilities
  B3.2 Feasibility and credibility of the project, including work plan
  B3.3 Management: Practical arrangements for the implementation and management of the research project**

B4 IMPACT (MAXIMUM 5 PAGES)

    B4.1 Contribution to research excellence by attracting and retaining first class researchers

    B4.2 Potential and quality of the researcher's long term professional integration in Europe

    B4.3 Potential of transferring knowledge to the host organisation

    B4.4 Capacity to develop lasting co-operation and collaborations with other countries

    B4.5 Plans for dissemination and exploitation of results development

    B4.6 Impact of the proposed outreach activities

B5 ETHICAL ISSUES – (NO PAGE LIMIT)

BIBLIOGRAPHY

END PAGE

  * Sub-criteria to be developed in the light of the principles of the 'European Charter for Researchers' and the 'Code of Conduct for the Recruitment of Researchers'.

** Any leave of absence of more than one year such as maternity/parental leave, sick or family care leave, military service, humanitarian aid work, etc. will be taken into account.

---

7 Look through the text again. What language feature do all the items have in common?

8 What might the *ethical issues* section be about? Note down your predictions. (You will need them later.)

Vocabulary focus

9 Read Text E again. It includes a large number of abstract nouns.

1 Why do you think there are so many abstract nouns in this text?

2 Many abstract nouns are formed by adding a suffix to a noun, verb or adjective. Complete the table below with nouns from the text. (Check the meaning of unknown words in the dictionary.)

3 Which are formed from nouns, which from verbs, and which from adjectives?

4 In pairs, compare your tables.

-ness	appropriateness, …
-ity	
-ology	
-ship	
-ence	
-ance	
-tion	
-ment	

10 Work in pairs or small groups. Imagine that you are going to submit a proposal. Discuss which section would seem most challenging to write up. Explain why you think so.

Reading focus 3

11 Work in pairs. Read the first paragraph of Text F.

1 Choose the best word/expression in options 1–9.
2 Explain your choice.

12 Read the whole of Text F to check the predictions you made in Activity 8. Say if they were correct.

F

> # ETHICAL ISSUES
>
> Ethics is (1) *very important/central* to scientific integrity, honesty and clarity of science. It is (2) *considered/seen as* essential by the REA and the European Commission in the research activities that it (3) *pays for/funds* or carries out itself. This means that in any proposal (4) *sent/submitted* to the 7th Framework programme, ethics issues must be identified and addressed. Proposals that (5) *put/pose* ethics (6) *concerns/worries* will be flagged. If some aspects are (7) *unfinished/incomplete*, clarification may be (8) *sought/asked for*, but this will (9) *cause/bring about* delays in the application process.
>
> Considering ethics issues from the concept stage of a proposal enhances the quality of research.
>
> Applicants should take time to consider the benefit/burden balance of the research activities; consider the impact of the research, not only in terms of scientific advancement, but also in terms of human dignity and social and cultural impact; consider elements such as the ethics and social impact of the research and whether there is a balance between the objectives and the means.

13 Work in pairs on Text F.

1 Identify and write down the key words that can help you summarise the text.
2 Now work on your own to explain the gist of the text in one or two sentences.
3 Compare sentences with your partner. Choose the one which expresses the main idea better. If necessary, improve it.

Reading focus 4

14 Read Text G and make a flow chart showing the sequence of negotiation. Compare your charts in pairs or small groups.

G

The Project Phase

Successful proposals will be invited to enter into negotiation. On the basis of the information provided, a 'grant agreement' is prepared and sent to the host organisation ('beneficiary'). The grant agreement should be signed in duplicate and returned to the Research Executive Agency for signature. Before the project starts, the host organisation signs an employment contract ('agreement') with the selected fellow in line with the provisions of the grant agreement. The start of the project will normally take place after the grant agreement enters into force, i.e. after its signature by the Research Executive Agency. *Exceptionally*, the start date of the project can be fixed retroactively (a date prior to the signature of the grant agreement) at the request of the host organisation and the researcher, *but at their own risk in case the negotiations fail.*

15 What is the function of *italics* in this text?

Follow-up

16 Reading texts about grants on the internet.

1 Search the internet and find a grant-giving scheme/programme that you would be interested in participating in.
2 Which criteria did you use to make your choice? Write them down.
3 Analyse the information and structure your notes according to the criteria.
4 Give a brief report to the group on your chosen programme and your reasons for choosing it.

Listening

In this module you will:

- listen to a range of formal and informal academic situations

- develop your ability to listen effectively for different purposes

Unit 1 Attending a conference

By the end of this unit you will be able to

⇒ use a variety of clues to predict the language and the content of listening

⇒ extract specific information from short conversations at an arrivals hall and at a hotel reception desk

Lesson 1 Arrival

Lead-in

1 Look at the picture. What problem do you think the traveller has? Have you ever had this problem at an international airport?

2 Work in pairs. Why might nobody have come to meet the traveller? Make a list of ideas.

The car is stuck in a traffic jam.

Language focus

3 Look at the list of language functions a–f. What phrases can you use to greet, introduce yourself, etc.?

a greeting and introducing   *Hello, my name is ...*   **d** asking for instructions
b asking for information   **e** giving polite instructions
c giving information   **f** making a request

4 ⊙2 **Complete these sentences from six conversations. Then listen and check.**

1 Hello, _____'s Kate Cornfield here.
2 I'm just _____ how to get to the conference.
3 I'll go to Terminal 1 and wait there, _____ I?
4 I'm just wondering _____ I should do.
5 Could you please _____ _____ a minute?
6 There _____ _____ to be anyone here to pick me up.
7 I'm just wondering _____ I _____ go.
8 _____ you _____ me where the taxi rank is?
9 How _____ I _____ you?
10 Someone was _____ to meet me at the bus station.
11 If you'll _____ for _____, I'll find _____ what the problem _____ .
12 _____ you wait a little _____ longer?
13 I've _____ _____ that the taxi broke _____ on the motorway.

5 **Match sentences 1–13 in Activity 4 with functions a–f in Activity 3.**

Strategy focus

6 **Answer the questions. Then identify the type of prediction in the conclusion about listening strategies.**

1 What did you predict in Activities 1 and 2?
2 What did you predict in Activity 3? How accurate was your prediction in terms of content and in terms of language?
3 What helped you to complete the gaps in Activity 4?
4 What is the purpose of Activity 5?
5 Did these activities help you listen? Why / Why not?

> Before listening we normally make predictions. We usually predict content and language.
>
> [1]_____ prediction: we guess the possible content of listening based on our background/ general knowledge of the world, knowledge of the culture or some subject knowledge.
>
> [2]_____ predictions: we guess the possible words, phrases that we might hear, based on the context/situation.

Skill development focus

7 ⊙3 **Listen to six conversations at an arrivals hall and tick the problem each person has. Give evidence.**

	Kate	Adam	Tasha	Tamara	Bolek	Reiko
1 The car is stuck in a traffic jam.						
2 The car is delayed because of a road accident.						
3 The car has broken down.						
4 The driver is at a different terminal.						
5 The traveller is in the wrong place.						
6 The driver is late as he got the time wrong.						

8 ⊙3 **Listen again. Are the statements below true (T), false (F) or there is no information given (NG)? Correct the false statements.**

1 Kate Cornfield should find the driver in Terminal 2. ____
2 Adam Murray doesn't agree to wait for the driver. ____
3 Tasha Blueberry should get a bus at the main entrance. ____
4 Tamara Orlova's flight has been delayed. ____
5 Bolek Grabowski is going to wait for a driver in a café. ____
6 Reiko Taketo has to wait 10 minutes before her taxi arrives. ____

Follow-up

9 ⊙4 **Listen to three conversations at an arrivals hall. Some responses are missing in the conversations. You will hear a number for each gap (1–8). Write the number of the gap next to the appropriate response (a–k).**

Conversation 1
a OK. Thanks. ____
b It's Hank Bright here. ____
c Yes, you can. ____
d There doesn't seem to be anyone to pick me up. ____

Conversation 2
e Yes, you may. ____
f Could you please hold on a minute? ____
g Speaking. How can I help you? ____

Conversation 3
h OK. Thanks. Sounds good. ____
i Hello. Can I speak to Julia Gassings please? ____
j OK, can you tell me where the taxi rank is? ____
k Hello. It's Julia Gassings here. ____

10 ⊙5 **Listen to the complete conversations and check your answers to Activity 9.**

11 ⊙5 **Listen again. Are the statements below true (T), false (F) or there is no information given (NG)?**

1 Hank Bright has just arrived at the airport. ____
2 Hank Bright should wait for the driver at Terminal 1. ____
3 Bartley Brown agrees to wait for the driver. ____
4 The taxi sent for Julia Gassings is in a traffic jam. ____
5 Julia Gassings doesn't know where the taxi rank is. ____
6 Julia Gassings will pay for the taxi by credit card. ____

12 ⊙4 **Listen again to the conversations with gaps from Activity 9. When you hear the gap, say what is missing.**

Lesson 2 Welcome to the Grand Hotel

Lead-in

1 **Look at the picture and make a list of things a traveller typically asks for or is asked about at a hotel reception desk.**

Language focus

2 Explain the underlined words and phrases.

1 When you <u>give your details</u> you *state your name, address and other personal information as required.*
2 When you <u>sign</u> something you …
3 When you say <u>I'm just wondering</u> you are going …
4 When you ask if something is <u>available</u> you want to know …
5 When someone <u>makes a booking</u> they …
6 If there is an <u>extra charge</u>, it means you …
7 You <u>check out</u> when …
8 You <u>need directions</u> when you have lost …

Skill development focus

3 ⊙ 6 **Work in pairs. Decide how to complete the phrases and who might say them: a receptionist (R) or a traveller (T). Then listen to a conversation at a hotel reception desk and check your ideas.**

1 Welcome _____ _____ Grand Hotel.
2 Could you fill out _____ _____ with your _____ and car registration _____, please?
3 I'm just wondering if there's access to _____ _____ in the _____.
4 You can pay for it when checking _____, with _____ or _____ _____.
5 Does your restaurant here serve _____ _____?
6 There are _____ to all the conference meeting rooms.

4 ⊙ 6 **Listen to the conversation again and tick the information the traveller requests.**

1 How to use the key card.
2 What hotel rules he must follow.
3 If he can use the internet in his room.

4 If the business centre is available at night.
5 If he will have to pay for using the business facilities.
6 How he can pay for extra services.
7 If there is a vegetarian restaurant.
8 How to find the meeting room.

Strategy focus

5 ⊙7 Read the extracts and say which are requests for information. Then listen and check.

1 There are a few things you should know about the hotel.
2 I'm wondering if there is wi-fi in my room.
3 Do you have an ironing room?
4 If you call Housekeeping, they'll do it for you.
5 There is a café in the hotel, isn't there?
6 I saw the sign for the gym.

6 Answer the questions.

1 What are the different ways of asking for information?
2 How do you know that it is a request in each case?
3 Complete the information below about strategies for listening for detail. Use the words from the list below. There is one word you do not need.

who question context rising wondering falling requested language

Before listening for detail we first make **1**_____ and **2**_____ predictions.
Then we pay attention to **3**_____ is speaking and how information is **4**_____ .
A request can be in the form of a **5**_____ , a statement with a **6**_____ tone or it can start with a phrase signalling a request (e.g. *I'm* **7**_____).

Follow-up

7 ⊙7 Listen to the conversation in Activity 5 again and write down three more requests.

8 ⊙6 Listen to the conversation in Activity 4 again and write down the exact phrases for the requests.

Follow the steps below.

1 Think of possible phrases before you listen.
2 Listen to the whole conversation and make a note of the phrases while listening. Do not stop listening even if you miss something.
3 When the recording is over, write down the words which you didn't write while listening.
4 Then, listen to the conversation with a pause after the missing phrases.
5 Check, add to and correct your notes.

Lesson 3 I seem to have a problem

Lead-in

1 Look at the list of the Grand Hotel room facilities and say which you are likely to use when you stay in a hotel. Why?

Room facilities

- Personal safe
- Laundry and dry-cleaning service
- Shoe-shine service
- High-speed wireless internet access
- Telephone
- Flat-screen LCD TV
- Fully stocked mini-bar
- Electronic door locks
- Room service

safe /seɪf/ noun [C] a strong box or cupboard with special locks where valuable things, especially money or jewels are kept

laundry /'lɔːndri/ noun [U] clothes, sheets, etc. that need to be washed: *to do the laundry; a laundry basket*

dry cleaning a shop where clothes are cleaned with chemicals

stock (v) to fill something such as a cupboard or shelves with food or goods

2 Tick the situations in which you need to call the receptionist from your hotel room.

1 You want to order lunch in your room.
2 You want nobody to disturb you.
3 You want to have your laundry done.
4 You cannot get into your room.
5 There is no water in your room.
6 You have problems with internet access.
7 You want to order a taxi.

Skill development focus

3 ⊙8 Listen to extracts from three conversations with a hotel receptionist. Match a speaker (A, B or C) to one of the problems (1–5) below.

The guest ...

1 wants to order lunch in his/her room.
2 wants to have his/her clothes washed.
3 cannot get into his/her room.
4 needs access to the internet.
5 wants to order a taxi.

4 What could a receptionist do to help the guests (A, B or C in Activity 3)?

Listening for relevant information

5 ⊙9 Work in three groups. Your teacher will give each group a different set of tasks (A, B or C). Listen to three conversations and do the tasks on your card.

Follow the steps:

1 Read the questions and the options on the card.
2 Get ready to note down a room number.
3 Listen to the conversation and tick the correct options on your card.
4 Check your answers with your group.

6 Work in new groups (A+B+C) and complete the other two cards. Don't show your card to the other people in your group but share the information.

7 Work in the same groups (A+B+C) and answer the questions below.

1 Who gets immediate help?
2 Who is staying on the eighth floor?
3 Who gets detailed instructions on what to do?
4 Who is told of a possible cause of the problem?

Strategy focus

8 Read the tips for listening for relevant information. Do you agree with them? Which activities did you use the strategies in?

To be successful in listening for relevant information you should …
1 read the task and make predictions.
2 check your predictions while listening.
3 decide on what information is important.
4 try to catch every single word.
5 listen for the information required by the task.
6 try to understand everything the first time you listen.

Follow-up

9 ⊙10 Listen to the conversations and answer the questions.

1 What problem does each guest have?
2 What is the solution to the problem?

10 ⊙11 Read the options for the guest's replies. Listen to what the receptionist says. Choose the guest's reply from the options and say it in the pause. Then listen and check.

1 **Guest:** *Thank you, not at all. / No, there's no connection at all. / Very slowly.*
2 **Guest:** *I just checked my email in the morning. / No, only for an hour. / Yes, all morning.*
3 **Guest:** *Yes, how much is it? / Yes, how many hours of free internet can I have? / Yes, how much is the game?*
4 **Guest:** *OK, I see. €16 per hour. / OK, I know. / OK. Do I have to pay now?*
5 **Guest:** *That's fine. / What do you do? / Oh, that's a pity.*

Unit 2 Troubleshooting

By the end of this unit you will be able to

➠ use a variety of clues to predict the content of listening

➠ recognise the communicative functions of utterances according to situations, participants and goals

➠ extract specific and detailed information

➠ infer the meaning of unknown words in a listening text

Lesson 1 Is there any technical help?

Lead-in

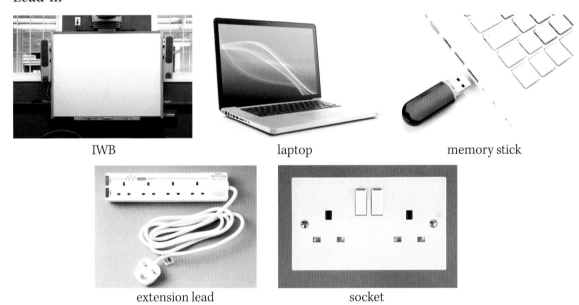

IWB   laptop   memory stick

extension lead   socket

1 Look at the pictures and answer the questions below.

1 What problem do you think a presenter might have with this equipment?
2 What other equipment might a presenter have a problem with? Make a list.
2 Have you ever had problems as a presenter at a conference?
3 Who usually helps you?

Language focus

2 Match the verbs to the objects in Activity 1. Make a list of all possible phrases.

1 to stop working	**6** to recognise	**11** to save something on
2 to set up	**7** to plug in	**12** to reboot
3 to use	**8** to put in	**13** to connect up
4 to show	**9** to have got a virus	**14** to switch on/off
5 to have a picture on	**10** to check	

3 ⊙ 12 You are going to hear some short situations with phrases from Activity 2. Listen and tick the phrases you hear.

Skill development focus

4 ⊙13 Listen to a conversation that takes place a few minutes before a presentation starts. When you hear a beep, predict what you will hear next. Then continue listening and check.

5 ⊙14 Listen to phrases 1–6 and match them to functions a–f.

a checking someone is the right person to help with a problem ____
b asking for help ____
c showing willingness (readiness) to help ____
d detecting/solving a problem ____
e expressing gratitude (thanks) ____
f responding to thanks ____

6 ⊙14 Listen again and complete the sentences below.

1 I'll see _____ .
2 _____ the IT _____ ?
3 My _____ .
4 _____ the connections. There might be a _____ . We _____ to use another socket. OK, I'll _____ .
5 Can you have _____ for me?
6 Thanks. I really appreciate _____ .

7 ⊙15 Listen to another conversation. Which of the functions from Activity 5 does the speaker use? Write down the order of the functions in the conversation.

8 ⊙15 Complete this report, written by the person in charge of the presentation equipment. Then listen and check.

A presenter asked me ¹_____ her presentation. It wasn't on the list of ²_____ but I lent her my laptop. The presenter couldn't ³_____ , so asked an IT technician ⁴_____ for her.

Strategy focus

9 Complete the questions below.

Before listening, we normally make predictions and then we check them as we hear. However, there may also be points where the conversation changes. So, it is important to ask yourself these questions.

1 Did I _____ that right?
2 Did I _____ what the speaker meant?
3 _____ did the speaker say that?
4 What will the speaker say _____ ?
5 Did the speaker _____ the topic?

Follow-up

10 ⊙16 Listen to a conversation at a conference. When you hear a beep, predict what you will hear next. Then continue listening and check your ideas.

11 ⊙16 Listen to the conversation again. Are the statements below true (T) or false (F)?

1 The presenter started the presentation ten minutes ago.
2 There is a problem with the memory stick.
3 The IT technician solved the problem by changing the leads.
4 The presenter needs a backup because the laptop has a virus.
5 The presenter asks for internet access to open the presentation.
6 The presenter needs a password to log on to the internet.
7 The presentation started later than scheduled.

12 ⊙16 Listen again and complete the statements.

Problem	1 The laptop _____ _____ _____ _____ _____ .
The technician's advice	2 We'll use _____ _____ .
	3 Let's just _____ _____ _____ _____ .
	4 We'll _____ _____ _____ _____ .
	5 Let me just _____ _____ _____ _____ _____ .
Result	6 You've _____ _____ _____ !
Attempt to solve the problem	7 Do you have another _____ _____ _____ _____ for your _____ ?
	8 Is there _____ _____ _____ in this room?
	9 You can _____ _____ _____ our network.
Solving the problem	10 I'm just _____ _____ _____ _____ .
	11 It's just _____ _____ .
Apologising	12 I'm really _____ _____ _____ _____ in starting the presentation.

Lesson 2 Are you in charge?

Lead-in

1 ⦿17 **Read the statements below about Interactive White Boards (IWBs). Then listen to what some teachers (1–3) say and match their opinions to the statements (a–c).**

a An IWB provides access to a vast library of resources for instruction and the added feature of interactivity.
b Those who embrace new technology have a powerful tool at their fingertips.
c An IWB is interactive only if a highly qualified teacher uses it.

2 Work in pairs and discuss the questions below.

1 Which teacher's opinion do you agree with most? Why?
2 What do you use an IWB for?
3 Have you ever had technical problems with an IWB? What happened?
4 What other technical problems might you have with an IWB?

Listening for specific information

3 ⦿18 **Listen to the beginning of a conversation that takes place before a presentation starts. Answer the questions.**

1 Has the presenter found the person in charge of the room?
2 What is the problem in the room?
3 How much time does the presenter have to prepare for the presentation?
4 Has the person in charge made the IWB work?

4 What do you think the person in charge will suggest next? Make a list of ideas.

5 ⦿18 **Listen to the end of the conversation and check your ideas.**

6 You are going to listen to a conversation where a presenter has a problem with the laptop. What are some common problems people have with computers and laptops?

7 ⦿19 **Listen to the beginning of another conversation and say what problem the presenter has.**

8 ⊙ 19 Listen to the whole conversation and complete the chart.

1	what the person in charge does
2	what the presenter asks for
3	what the person in charge does this time
4	who helps the presenter
5	why they ask the audience to wait for a couple of minutes

Strategy focus

9 ⊙ 20 Listen to this extract from the conversation and do the tasks below.

1 Complete the phrase: *we* _____ *hitch*
2 What will happen after the action in *1*?
3 What type of word is *hitch*?
4 Choose the best meaning for *hitch* (a, b, c or d) in this situation.
   a a device for a presentation
   b a temporary difficulty that causes a short delay
   c a small problem
   d a complicated problem

10 Decide whether the following statements are true (T) or false (F).

> To infer the meaning of an unknown word you should:
> **1** get an idea of what the extract you are listening to is about.
> **2** identify the context around the unknown word.
> **3** identify the type of word, or function, of the unknown word.

Follow-up

11 ⊙ 18 Read the statements below. Write down what you think the person on the recording said in each of these situations. Then listen and check your ideas.

Someone ...
1 wants to know if a specific person is in charge of the room.
2 wants to know what to do if there is a problem with the equipment in the room..
3 wants to know if a presentation is starting soon.
4 says that they can't help.
5 says that they can't work without an IWB.
6 wants to know if the presenter will agree to change the room.
7 says that they approve of an idea.
8 asks the person in charge to inform late participants about a room change.
9 agrees to help.

Lesson 3 Is the problem solved?

Lead-in

1 Look at the pictures and answer the questions.

1 What problem do you think each presenter has?
2 How can it be solved?

2 Work in pairs. Act out a short conversation between a presenter and a person in charge, based on the pictures.

Listening for specific information

3 ⊙21 Listen to two conversations at a conference. Complete the table below while listening.

	object	problem	solution	who helped
1				
2				

4 Make a list of possible technical problems at a conference. Complete the spidergram.

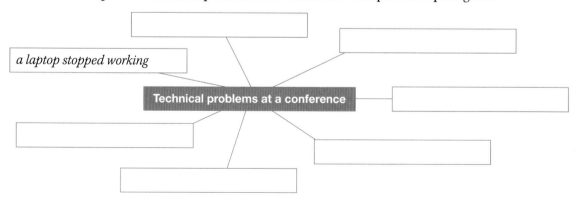

a laptop stopped working

Technical problems at a conference

5 Work in two groups.

Group 1: You are presenters. Prepare to find the person in charge, ask for help and tell them about the problem. Discuss all the problems in Activity 4.

Group 2: You are the person in charge. Prepare to suggest possible solutions to the problems in Activity 4.

6 Work in pairs (a presenter and a person in charge). Your teacher will give you a problem from Activity 4. Discuss the problem.

7 Take turns to act out your problems from Activity 6 in front of the group. Complete the chart below while listening to the other groups.

	object	problem	solution
1			
2			

Follow-up

8 ⊙21 Listen to the conversations in Activity 3 again and write down exact phrases the speakers use to express the following functions.

	Conversation 1	Conversation 2
explaining the problem		
asking for help		
agreeing to help		
explaining the situation		
approving of the actions of the person in charge		
thanking the person for their help		

73

Lesson 4 Good news … Bad news …

Lead-in

1 When do you usually do the following: before or during a conference? Put ticks in the table.

	before	during
register at a conference		
pay the conference fee		
register for a social event		
register for a session		

2 At conferences, you often hear announcements. Discuss the questions in pairs and be ready to share your ideas with the group.

1 What are conference announcements usually about?
2 Is it easy or difficult to understand the information you need? Why?
3 Some people say that numbers are the most difficult to understand while listening. Do you agree?

Language focus

3 ⊙22 Listen and choose the numbers you hear twice.

1 12/20　　**2** 13/30　　**3** 14/40　　**4** 15/50　　**5** 16/60　　**6** 17/70　　**7** 18/80　　**8** 19/90

Strategy focus

4 ⊙23 Listen to the announcements and work out the meaning of each word by answering the questions below.

1 _____ _____ _____ *fee*
   a Complete the phrase with the missing words.
   b What can be done with a *fee*?
   c Is *fee* a noun here?
   d What does *fee* mean?

2 _____ _____ _____ _____ *our treasurer*
   a Complete the phrase with the missing words.
   b What can a *treasurer* do?
   c What type of word is *treasurer*?
   d What does *treasurer* mean?

3 *postponement of the* _____ _____ _____
   a Complete the phrase with the missing words.
   b What happened to the speaker?
   c When was her talk planned?
   d Will she speak? When?
   e What does *postponement* mean?

4 *cancellation of today's* _____
   a Complete the phrase with the missing word.
   b What information might help you to understand this word?
   c What does *cancellation* mean?

Skill development focus

5 ⊙24 **Listen to five announcements at a conference venue and tick the purpose of each.**

purpose		1	2	3	4	5
a	to remind delegates about registration for participation in a session					
b	to tell the delegates about the change in the schedule of the conference					
c	to tell the delegates when and where they can pay the fee					
d	to inform the delegates about an after-conference event					
e	to inform the delegates that one of the events will not take place					

6 ⊙24 **Listen to announcements 1–4 in Activity 5 and fill in the gaps below.**

Announcement 1
1 The last day for payment is Thursday, _____.
2 The treasurer is in Room _____.

Announcement 2
3 Dr Bakar was to give his talk at _____ today.
4 The participants can listen to Dr Bakar the next day at _____.

Announcement 3
5 The tour bus leaves at _____ and returns at about _____.

Announcement 4
6 You have to sign up by _____ o'clock if the parallel sessions start at _____ o'clock, and by
  _____ o'clock if the parallel sessions start at _____ o'clock.

Follow-up

7 ⊙25 **Listen to three announcements and match each one to its purpose (a–h).**

Announcement 1

Announcement 2

Announcement 3

a to inform the delegates about a change in time
b to inform the delegates about the price of the dinner
c to inform the delegates about a change of place
d to tell the delegates about the venue for the dinner
e to tell the delegates about the opening of something
f to tell the delegates about the desk opening hours
g to tell the delegates about the menu of the dinner
h to inform the delegates about the conference dinner

8 ⊙25 **Listen to the three announcements again and do the tasks below.**

1 Announcement 1: correct the schedule below.

14.00	Parallel session 1	Reform in Engineering of European Countries	Room H203

2 Announcement 2: complete the information below.

Information desk opening hours			
Thursday	**Friday**	**Saturday**	**Sunday**
_____ - _____	_____ - _____	_____ - _____	_____ - _____

3 Announcement 3: answer the questions below.
  a What is the event?
  b When is the event? (day and time)
  c Who can the delegates bring along?
  d What is the price?

Unit 3 Networking

By the end of this unit you will be able to

⇒ extract specific information from short conversations while networking
⇒ recognise stress and rhythm in spoken English
⇒ identify key words in utterances
⇒ identify communicative functions of phrases while listening

Lesson 1 Have we met before?

Lead-in

1 ⊙26 **Listen to the beginning of a conversation between two people at a conference and answer the questions below.**

1 What event did they both take part in yesterday?
2 Are they talking in a very formal situation now?
3 Do you find both speakers equally easy to understand?

Language focus

2 ⊙27 **Listen to the beginning of another conversation between two people at a conference. Answer the questions.**

1 When does the conversation take place?
2 How does the man know about the woman's work?

3 ⊙27 **Listen to the conversation from Activity 2 again. Write down the sentences which support your answers. Then answer the questions.**

1 Which sentence refers to the time of the event both speakers attended? What verb form is used?
2 Which sentence describes the speaker's experience as important for the present? What verb form is used?
3 Which verb form is easier to hear? Why?

Skill development focus

4 ⊙28 **Look at the full and contracted forms in the box. Then listen and complete the sentences with the correct contracted forms.**

Full form	have	is	was not	would	will	did not
Contracted form	've	's	wasn't	'd	'll	didn't

1 I _____ had a lot to do.
2 How _____ the conference going for you?
3 Well, sorry I _____ there to see you.
4 What _____ your area of expertise?
5 And I _____ got an abstract as well which you could have.

6 I _____ had to cancel the meeting.
7 I _____ really appreciate that.
8 I _____ go for the first method.
9 Sorry, I _____ hear about that.

Strategy focus

5 ⊙29 Every speaker is unique. Listen to eight utterances and match them with their standard written form (a–h). The first one is done for you.

_____ **a** How are you?

_____ **b** Very well, thanks.

___1___ **c** Yes, I was. I don't know if ...

_____ **d** I think you were at my presentation yesterday, weren't you?

_____ **e** Fine, thanks. And how's the conference going for you?

_____ **f** You know, I'm a great admirer of your work and the presentation really impressed me.

_____ **g** I wonder if we could perhaps meet up later on to discuss ...

_____ **h** Hello, it's Alan, isn't it?

6 ⊙30 Order the sentences in Activity 5 to make a conversation. Then listen and check. Role-play the conversation.

7 Answer the questions about the utterances in Activity 5.

1 What is noticeable about the words *conference* and *perhaps* in the way the speaker pronounces them?

2 What is noticeable about the phrase *admirer of*?

8 What can help you identify words in continuous speech? Tick the options you agree with.

1 Rely on consonants.

2 Reconstruct the words from context.

3 If accents are used, establish similarities with and differences from standard written English.

4 Ask your partner to speak more slowly.

5 Avoid communication.

Listening for specific information

9 ⊙31 Listen to the beginning of three conversations. Write down the initial phrases of each first speaker.

10 ⊙31 Listen again to the conversations from Activity 9. Make notes in the table.

	Who are the speakers? (personal details: e.g. names, country/city)	Where/When does the conversation take place?	Where/When did the speakers see each other before?
Conversation 1			
Conversation 2			
Conversation 3			

Follow-up

11 ⊙32 Listen to five sentences and write them down.

12 ⊙33 Order the sentences in Activity 11 to make a conversation. Then listen and check.

Lesson 2 What did you think of it?

Lead-in

1 ⊙34 **Listen to an extract from a conversation between two people at a conference and answer the questions.**

1 What does the woman think of the conference?
2 What does the man think about his talk at the conference?
3 Are these opinions easy to understand? Why? Why not?

Language focus

2 Study the examples of noun phrases below. Underline the head noun in each example.

1 An interesting <u>workshop.</u>
2 The workshop on project development.
3 The workshop by O'Brien.
4 The students' presentation.
5 An online learning performance case study.

3 ⊙35 **Listen to the noun phrases from Activity 2. Write down the word which is most important for the speaker (the key word) in each of them.**

1 interesting

4 Answer the questions.

1 What helped you to detect the key words in Activity 3?
2 Are they the same as the head nouns in Activity 2?

5 ⊙36 **Listen and complete the sentences with the missing noun phrases.**

1 It was _____ _____ _____ _____ _____ , wasn't it?
2 Do you mean the _____ _____ _____ _____ _____ _____ _____ _____ _____
   _____ ?
3 What did you think of _____ _____ _____ _____ _____ ?
4 They have to sessions that look quite interesting to me. One's on _____ _____ _____
   _____ _____ .
5 And the other is _____ _____ _____ _____ _____ .

6 ⊙36 **Listen to the statements from Activity 5 again and write down the key words. More than one key word in a noun phrase is possible.**

1 project

Skill development focus

7 Read the incomplete sentence below and answer the questions.

The presentation is about ...

1 Does the sentence make sense? Why / Why not?
2 Why is it important to understand what part of a sentence contains the key information?

8 Say the statements below one at a time and complete them in your own way. Then listen to your teacher say versions of the same statements, repeat them and develop them further. Repeat this until you get to the end of each statement.

1 The presentation is about ...
2 It was one of those presentations where ...
3 I came out ...

Strategy focus

9 What helps you to identify key words when someone is speaking? Tick the correct options below. Give reasons.

1 sentence stress
2 repetition of the word
3 position of the word in the sentence
4 structure of the sentence
5 type of word (verb, noun, adjective, etc.)
6 context
7 the speaker's behaviour

Listening for opinions

10 ⊙37 Listen to an extract from a conversation. Identify the key words the man uses to express his opinion.

11 Answer the questions about the conversation from Activity 10.

1 Is the man's opinion positive or negative? How do you know?
2 What helped you identify the key words?

12 ⊙38 Listen to another conversation and make notes in the table about what the speakers liked and disliked about the presentation.

	liked about the presentation	disliked about the presentation
man		
woman		

Follow-up

13 ⊙39 Listen to another extract from a conversation where a woman expresses her opinion. Make a note of the key words she uses.

14 ⊙40 Listen to another conversation and answer the questions.

1 Who is the presentation by?
2 What is it about?
3 Did the speakers like or dislike the presentation? Why?

Lesson 3 What we'll do ...

Lead-in

1 How do people develop professional contacts at conferences? Make a list of possible arrangements they make.

2 ⊙41 Listen to a conversation about arrangements and answer the questions.

1 What will the man do?
2 What will the woman do?
3 What helped you understand the conversation?
4 Was anything difficult?

Skill development focus

3 ⊙42 Listen to what a speaker says while making an arrangement and answer the questions.

1 Is the way the speaker expresses his idea long or short?
2 Does he make all the words/phrases sound equally important?

4 ⊙42 Listen again. Write down the words/phrases which are important for the listener who is making an arrangement with the speaker.

what we'll do ...

5 ⊙43 Listen and underline the stressed syllables in the sentences below. Then answer questions 1 and 2.

a Er ... I'd be <u>inclined</u> to go to the session on the gender case study, the comparative gender case study.
b Er ..., but you know, the learning styles one ... you can catch up on the research in the presenter's articles.
c Well, er ... It was not really my area of interest ... not really my area of expertise, but I was really interested in the topic.

1 What words are stressed by the speakers?
2 What type of words are they (nouns, verbs, adjectives, pronouns)?

6 ⊙43 Listen again. Tap on the table in time with the stressed words.

1 What did you notice about the intervals between the stressed syllables?
2 How can rhythm and stress help you identify key words while listening?

Strategy focus

7 Complete the statement about how to identify key words in an utterance. You don't need to use all the words.

more important	less important	rhythm	stress	stressed	Unstressed	equal	unequal

---

How to identify key words in spoken English

There are some words in what a speaker says which are [1]_____ for the listener than the speaker. [2]_____ and [3]_____ of spoken English help to identify the key words. The [4]_____ words are more important for understanding key ideas in an utterance. They appear in speech after [5]_____ intervals. [6]_____ words 'stick' to the stressed ones. We can guess the unstressed words from the context.

---

8 ⊙44 Listen to what two speakers say while making an arrangement. Write down the key words which are important for the listener.

Speaker 1 interested more about, ...

Listening for specific information

9 ⊙45 Listen to extracts from two conversations in which the speakers are making arrangements. Make notes in the table.

	What do the speakers agree to do?	When?	Why?
1			
2			

Follow-up

10 ⊙46 Listen to two conversations between speakers who were at the same event, but did not have a chance to speak. Tick the functions the speakers use.

		1	2
1	initiating a conversation		
2	referring to the context of the previous meeting		
3	introducing oneself		
4	asking for opinion		
5	expressing opinion		
6	changing the topic		
7	making arrangements for the future (suggestion/request)		
8	asking for clarification		
9	confirming information		

11 ⊙46 Listen again. Write down an example for each function in Activity 10.

Initiating a conversation – Oh, hello, Stuart. How are you?

Lesson 4 Can we talk?

Lead-in

1 Do you agree with the idea 'politeness is an international concept'? Why / Why not?

Language focus

2 How can you start a conversation at a professional event with a person you do not know? Tick the functions below and think of example phrases.

1 initiating the conversation with a polite request
2 giving details about your job
3 paying a compliment
4 asking for advice
5 stating the purpose of the conversation
6 apologising

3 ⊙47 Listen to the beginning of a conversation after a conference and decide if the statements below are true (T) or false (F).

1 The speakers know each other well. ___
2 The man starts the conversation. ___
3 The man pays the presenter a compliment. ___
4 The man wants to talk to the presenter because she also works at a university. ___
5 The man wants the government to support his research. ___
6 The man feels it is all right if he asks the presenter for feedback on his research. ___

4 ⊙47 Listen again and fill in the missing words in the phrases below.

1 Could I have _____ with you, please?
2 I just heard your presentation. It was _____, very inspirational. I _____ enjoyed it. And I learned a lot.
3 I'm a researcher and I work at a _____.
4 And actually that's one of the reasons I wanted _____ to you because I saw you've done a lot of work with the government through your _____. And that's something I want to do.
5 Could you give me some _____?
6 I'm sorry if I'm _____ you.

5 Identify the functions of the phrases in Activity 4. Use the list in Activity 2 to help you.

Listening for relevant information

6 Make predictions about the way the conversation might develop. Complete the phrase below with what could help to win government support for research.

First of all, you have to have some really good ...

7 ⊙48 Listen to the main part of the conversation. Check your predictions for Activity 6 and choose the right answers for the questions below.

1 The woman advises the man to start by
   a approaching the government.
   b collecting statistical evidence.
   c having some really good qualitative research.

2 The woman believes that the most difficult task in winning government support is
   a getting close to governments.
   b lobbying governments.
   c choosing the right person to lobby.

3 According to the woman's experience, the best way to approach governments is by
   a phoning people.
   b emailing people.
   c developing networks.
   d inviting people to attend conferences.

8 ⊙49 **Listen to the end of the conversation. Choose the correct options in each conclusion. Give evidence for your choice.**

Conclusion 1

The man *is not persistent / quite persistent* with his request. The man *sounds polite / does not sound polite*. The man *feels / does not feel* comfortable about his request.

Conclusion 2

The woman is *polite / not polite*. The woman *agrees to read the whole paper / explains to what extent she is ready to help*.

Conclusion 3

When the woman agrees to help, the man responds *with thanks / by showing how happy he is*.

Follow-up

9 ⊙48 **Listen to the conversation from Activity 7 again. Write down the phrases which are close in meaning to the following words/phrases.**

1 evidence
2 the right solution to the problem
3 to think things over

10 ⊙49 **Listen to the conversation from Activity 8 again and complete the phrases below.**

making a request	responding to a request politely
1 I have _____ _____ _____ _____.	**1** I'll _____ if I _____.
2 _____ _____ send you my research?	**2** Well, I'_____ _____ _____ in an abstract ...
3 _____ _____ _____ just point me in the right direction for my research.	**3** I'll _____. I'd be ... interested to see it and _____ to learn _____ _____ the background of the work...

11 ⊙49 **Listen again. Write down an example phrase for each of the functions below.**

1 exchanging contacts *Here's my card.*
2 thanking someone for something
3 saying goodbye at the end of a first conversation

Unit 4 In the audience

By the end of this unit you will be able to

➡ extract gist and specific information from oral presentations

➡ use a variety of strategies for listening to a presentation

Lesson 1 Your participation is welcome

Lead-in

1 What is the difference between a *lecture* and a *presentation*? Use the dictionary entries, your experience and the words and phrases in the box below to answer the question.

> **presentation** [/ˌprezən'teɪʃən/] n – [C] a formal talk in which you describe or explain something to a group of people: give/ make a presentation on something

> **lecture** [/'lektʃə(r)/] n – [C] a talk to a group of people about a particular subject, at college or university: give a lecture on something

length	visual support
students	university teachers
lecturers	administrators
managers	research
project	organisation
problem	interactive
relationship with audience	

Language focus

2 ⊙50 Listen to the explanations and make a note of the meaning of the words below.

1 divide
2 overview
3 exactly

4 define
5 attempt
6 dimension

3 ⊙51 Complete the table. Then listen and tick the word you hear.

noun	verb
participation	
	welcome
	behave
	define
meaning	

4 ⊙52 Read the dictionary entries below. Then listen to speakers A and B and write down the phrases that contain these words. Do speakers A and B use the words with the same meaning? How do they differ?

> **general** [/'dʒenərəl/] adj. – not specific or detailed, describing only the main features

> **particular** [/pə'tɪkjələ(r)/] adj. – special, or this and not any other

> **addition** [/ə'dɪʃən/] n – something that has been added to something else

5 ⊙ 53 **Listen and identify how many words are missing in each sentence. Then listen again and complete the sentences.**

1 I'm going to divide ...
2 I'm going to make an effort ...
3 What do they mean ...?
4 You can see what STEM stands ...
5 What are the pressures that they ...

Strategy focus

6 Work in pairs. Go through Activities 2–5 and match the sub skills below to the Activity you practised it in.

For effective listening we need to develop the following subskills:

a identifying when a familiar word is part of a prepositional phrase.
b identifying related words.
c noticing the unstressed parts in a phrase.
d identifying the functional difference between related words.
e relating what you hear to your previous knowledge.

Skill development focus

7 ⊙ 54 **Read these pairs of phrases and say how they differ. Then listen and tick the phrases you hear.**

1 **a** ... so many people here today from ...   **b** So, many people here today from ...
2 **a** I'm going to talk ...   **b** I'd been going to talk ...
3 **a** Thank you for coming along.   **b** Thank you for coming alone.
4 **a** a fix   **b** ethics
5 **a** I'm going to talk today about research   **b** I'm going to talk to you today about research
     ethics.   ethics.

8 Work in pairs. What part of the presentation did you hear in Activity 7: the start, the main part or the end? Give reasons.

9 ⊙ 55 **Read three extracts from presentations and decide what words are missing. Then listen and check your predictions. Which presentation would you prefer to go to? Why?**

1 I'm Ron Smithers and today _____ talk about how much scientists really know.
2 Good afternoon _____ . My name is Joanna Richards and my _____ the role of metaphors in science.
3 Well, in my presentation _____ I will try to answer the question: How is mathematics like a language? And I'm really glad _____ in the audience and I hope the presentation _____ to your expectations.

10 ⊙56 Listen to the presentation opener and complete the overview slide.

Presentation overview

1 What are _____ in general?

2 What are _____ in particular?

3 How different are research ethics in _____ and STEM (science, technology, engineering, mathematical) _____?

4 Why are some researchers sometimes _____?

5 What can you _____?

11 ⊙56 Look at the phrases below from the presentation opener. There is one mistake in each phrase. Listen and correct the mistakes.

1 I'm going to talk to you today about research methods and it's really nice …
2 Thank you for coming alone.
3 The talk will be about 50 minutes and I'm going to divide it into sections.
4 First, I'm going to try to divide ethics in general.
5   I'm not Aristophane, Socrates or a Greek philosopher, but I'm going to make an attempt to do that.
6 Them I'm going to focus on research ethics in particular: what exactly they are …
7 … STEM stands for the science, technology, engineering and methodology disciplines.
8 What are the pressures that they work after?
9 … and this is there your participation will be welcome.

12 Work in groups of three and prepare a presentation opener. You can use the following phrases to help you.

1 Today I'm going to talk to you about …
2 I'm going to divide the talk into …
3 First, I'm going to …
4 Then, I'm going to …
5 After that, I'm going to …
6 Finally, I'm going to …

13 Listen to your groupmate's presentation opener and write an overview slide.

Follow-up

14 ⊙57 Listen to the opener of another presentation and answer the questions.

1 What is the topic of the presentation?
2 How long will it take?
3 How many sections are there in the presentation?

Lesson 2 The three golden rules

Lead-in

1 Read the dictionary definition. You are going to hear the main part of a presentation on ethics. How do you think the topic might be connected to your field?

> **ethics** [/ˈeθɪks/] n [C usually plural] a system of accepted beliefs
>   which control behaviour, especially such a system based on morals

Skill development focus

2 ⊙58 Listen to a definition of ethics and write down the key words.

3 ⊙58 Choose the correct options to make phrases from the definition in Activity 2. Then listen and check.

1 conflict
   a there is a   **b** where is a   **c** it is a
2 do
   a that you   **b** what you   **c** how you
3 act
   a have you   **b** how you   **c** who you
4 believe
   a watch you   **b** what you   **c** that you
5 principles
   a your   **b** her   **c** the

4 Complete the extract below with the key words that make the definition understandable.

> It's something which comes into play when ¹_____ between ²_____ and ³_____ on the one hand, and ⁴_____ and ⁵_____ on the other hand.

5 Compare the definitions in Activities 1 and 4 and say how they are different.

6 ⊙59 Listen to the next part of the presentation and complete the missing information. What helped you identify it?

There are three different levels of ethics the speaker is going to look at:
1 the _____ level;
2 the _____ level;
3 the _____ level.

Strategy focus

7 Read the statements below and say whether you agree with them or not. Why / Why not? Give examples from Activities 2–6.

1 When you listen to a longer piece of speaking, it is important to identify key words.
2 Key words are usually stressed and pronounced more distinctly.
3 Unstressed words can often be inferred based on context and the key words.
4 Some English words/phrases can be easily confused. You need to practise understanding the differences between them.

Language focus

8 ⊙60 **Read the pairs of phrases. How are they different? Listen and tick the phrase you hear.**

1 a ethical rules which we ought to follow   **3 a** respect for
   b rules which govern ethics   **b** with respect to
2 a across all disciplines   **4 a** in a large society
   b a crossover of disciplines   **b** society at large

Listening for gist and for specific information

9 ⊙61 **Listen to what the speaker says about the three golden rules of research ethics and tick the most important key words/phrases used. Give reasons for your choice.**

The first rule	respect research subjects human participants object of research animals the environment conversations confidential anonymous
The second rule	truth honesty standards field of research individual researcher evidence hypothesis
The third rule	accuracy quality of knowledge the best tools and instruments collection of data

10 Which statement below sums up this part of the presentation best? Give reasons.

1 Research ethics ought to be applied on all three levels – personal, professional and legal – in any field of research.
2 There are three main rules that ought to be applied in any field of research.
3 Respect for human beings is the basis for research ethics in any field of research.

11 Express each of the three golden rules in one sentence. Use words from Activity 9.

Strategy focus

12 Which of the Activities (9–11) was aimed at listening for specific information?

Follow-up

13 ⊙61 **Listen to the talk again and make notes on the questions below.**

1 What is the most important example of research ethics in psychology?
2 What is the result of ethical behaviour in research?
3 What are the five things that make up 'accuracy in research' according to the speaker?

14 ⊙62 **Listen to the story and the discussion of unethical behaviour at one of the levels that the speaker mentions in Activity 6. What level is it? What 'golden rule' is broken?**

Lesson 3 A story to illustrate my point

Lead-in

1 What three 'golden rules' of research ethics did the presenter in Lesson 2 mention in his presentation? What do you think of them?

2 You are going to listen to a speaker talking about some reasons for unethical behavior in research. What do you think he will mention?

Skills development focus

3 ⦿ 63 Listen to short extracts from the presentation and tick the phrases you hear.

1 **a** Well, you, no!
   b Well, you know
   c Well, you, now
2 **a** in low courts
   b in low coats
   c in law courts
3 **a** they are
   b here are
   c there are

4 **a** many of you wear this
   b many of you are aware of this
   c many of you know where it is
5 **a** something is used
   b some of them is this
   c some of the issues
6 **a** They made tracks by the money.
   b They may be tractable, the money.
   c They may be attracted by the money.

4 ⦿ 64 Read the unfinished sentences and guess how they might end in the presentation. Then listen to the whole sentences and check your ideas.

1 Why are researchers sometimes ...
2 There can be conflicts ...
3 And in most countries – in Russia, in Britain, in the United States – big corporations ...
4 And sometimes the big corporations want certain results ...
5 The researchers may want ...
6 They may be tempted to ...
7 On the other hand, they lose ...
8 They lose the respect of ...
9 And there are cases which finish in ....

Listening for specific information

5 Think about what you heard in Activity 4 and answer the questions.

1 What reason(s) for unethical behaviour in research does the speaker mention?
2 What sort of unethical behaviour can this result in?

6 ⦿ 65 Work in groups (A, B and C). Listen to another part of the presentation and answer the questions.

Group A: What new reason(s) for unethical behaviour in research does the speaker mention here?
Group B: What example of unethical behaviour does the speaker focus on in this part?
Group C: Make notes on what the speaker says about this example of unethical behaviour.

7 ⊙66 **Listen to an example of an ethical dilemma in research and choose the correct options below. Give reasons.**

1 Professor Hardworking is
   a a real person whose name has been changed
   b a fictional character in a typical situation
   c a real name of a real person.
2 The research grant money was
   a spent rather poorly
   b spent very well
   c completely lost
3 In a major international journal, Professor Hardworking has published
   a many papers
   b several papers
   c just one paper
4 The research team from Singapore wants Professor Hardworking
   a to publish her set of newly collected data in their journal
   b to allow them to publish similar research
   c to allow them to use the results of her preliminary research
5 One of the conditions of the funding was that all the data Professor Hardworking collected should be made public. The speaker is
   a certain about this
   b not certain about this
   c doesn't mention this

8 **Explain Professor Hardworking's dilemma in a few sentences.**

Strategy focus

9 **Work in pairs and discuss the questions below.**

1 When do you have to listen for specific information?
2 What helps you to do it effectively?
3 How is listening for specific information different from listening for gist?

Follow-up

10 ⊙67 **Listen to an example offered by a member of the audience. Is it relevant to the presentation on research ethics? Why / Why not?**

11 ⊙67 **Listen again and complete the sentences.**

1 That makes me think of a story that happened in a _____ area of science...
2 Most people expected _____ names to be the winners.
3 Some of them seemed to really _____ each other.
4 One of the researchers had access to very good equipment to produce the best possible _____ images.
5 The others were capable of a _____ of imagination, so to speak.
6 I can't _____ feeling sad when ...

Lesson 4 And finally …

Lead-in

1 Work in pairs. Suggest three ways to complete this definition. Be ready to explain your ideas.

> Science is …
> 1 _____
> 2 _____
> 3 _____

Language focus

2 ⊙68 Read the sentences and guess the meaning of the underlined words. Then listen to the definitions and match them to the words in the sentences.

1 The natural sciences have <u>revealed</u> many truths about the world. ___
2 The 20th century was <u>remarkable</u> for its inventions. ___
3 The same method can be <u>applied</u> to other situations. ___
4 He used to <u>quote</u> this famous philosopher in all his public speeches. ___
5 The movie is based on the <u>true</u> story of a London gangster. ___
6 This diagram shows the indicators of change in the <u>state</u> of the environment. ___

3 ⊙69 What kind of information might come after the underlined words in the sentences? Choose from the options. Then listen and complete the sentences.

1 Appearances may lead us to believe that things are exactly as our eyes tell, <u>like</u> …
2 I could go on and on telling success stories of scientific discovery. <u>In other words</u> …
3 'Not to fool ourselves' means to be aware of the true state of things <u>despite</u> …

a something that you don't take into account
b something that provides the example to what is said in the first part
c something that expresses the idea in the first part but in different words

Skill development focus

4 ⊙70 Listen to Part 1 of a presentation and say how this beginning is different from the presentation on research ethics you heard in Lesson 2.

5 ⊙70 Listen to Part 1 again. Each time the teacher pauses the recording, say what the words below refer to. What helped you to understand in each case?

1 it   4 us
2 it   5 it
3 ourselves

6 ⊙70 Listen to Part 2 of the presentation and add correct punctuation in the extract below.

I could go on and on telling success stories of scientific discovery and how science revealed the true state of things in other words the history of science is a story of remarkable achievements so it is not surprising that this extraordinary success of the natural sciences has led some people to believe that it is the dominant cognitive paradigm or model of knowledge

7 ⊙70 Listen to Part 3 of the presentation and say which of the statements below is a quotation from Carl Sagan and which are interpretations by the speaker. How do you know?

Science is more ...
1 a method used in research than it is a result that we get by applying the method.
2 than a body of knowledge. It is a way of thinking ...
3 a way to get knowledge, rather than a set of truths we already know.

8 Work in groups of three. Sum up the content of Parts 1–3 of the presentation in a three sentences. Present your summary to the group.

9 ⊙70 Listen again and check your ideas.

Strategy focus

10 Revise the strategies a listener should use. Match the beginning to the end of each sentence.

1 Before listening ...
2 If I listen for gist ...
3 When I identify key words ...
4 If I do not know the word ...
5 If I cannot guess the meaning from the context ...
6 When I listen for specific information ...

a I pay attention to key words.
b I try to guess the meaning from the context.
c I try to identify its function (e.g. noun, verb, etc.)
d I make predictions about content and language.
e I pay attention to rhythm and stress.
f I identify what facts are required in the task.

Speaking

module 3

In this module you will:

- meet some common social situations
- develop your presentation skills

Unit 1 Socialising

By the end of this unit you will be able to

➡ introduce yourselves and others in formal and informal situations

➡ start a conversation and keep it going

➡ show interest and react to news

➡ invite people, accept or decline invitations

➡ pay and receive compliments

➡ thank people, apologise and say goodbye

Lesson 1 Greetings and introductions

Lead-in

Good morning, Ms Brown.

Good morning, Mr Smirnov. Welcome to the conference.

Oh, Marlene, glad you're here.

Hi, Bob. Nice to see you again.

I'm sorry. We haven't been introduced. My name is Doctor Linda Schulz from Dresden University.

Hey there, how are you doing, Linda? I'm Alex. First time in Zurich?

1 How do you greet people in formal and informal situations in your culture? How do you usually introduce yourself and others?

2 Work in pairs. Look at the pictures. How are they different? Which situation seems inappropriate? Why?

Formal and informal greetings

3 ⊙71 Listen to six conversations. They all take place at a conference. How well do the speakers know each other?

4 Work in pairs. Tick the best response (a, b or c) in each situation. Sometimes, more than one answer may be correct.

1

> During a coffee break Olaf Swenson sees his colleague from the Prague Business School.
>
> **Olaf:** Hello, Harry. Remember me? I'm Olaf Swenson.
> **Harry: a** I am glad to meet you too.
>   **b** Oh! Yes, of course. How are you?
>   **c** Hello, Olaf. Pleased to meet you.

2

> At the conference participants' registration table Peter meets Val. Val and Peter have met before at international conferences. Val wants to introduce Peter to his colleague Andrew.
>
> **Val:** Peter, this is Andrew Painter, a colleague of mine from Ashcroft Business School.
> **Peter: a** How are things?
>   **b** Nice to meet you. I'm Peter.
>   **c** Hello, Andrew. Nice to meet you.

3

> Roberta and Nick are talking during lunch time. They know each other very well.
>
> **Nick:** Hey, Roberta, how are things?
> **Roberta: a** I am pleased to meet you.
>   **b** Not bad. And you, Nick?
>   **c** Fine, thanks.

4

> You are at a conference in Cambridge and want to introduce yourself to Professor Compton, a well-known academic in the field of your research.
>
> **You:** You must be Professor Compton.
> **Professor Compton: a** Pleased to meet you.
>   **b** That's right! Why?
>   **c** Yes, that's me. What's your name?

5

> Simon and his Russian friend Alex are sitting in the café. Simon sees his British colleague Mike and introduces him to Alex.
>
> **Simon:** Do you know Mike? Mike, this is my friend Alex from Russia.
> **Alex: a** Hello, I'm pleased.
>   **b** No, I don't know Mike. I'm glad to meet him.
>   **c** Hello, Mike. Glad to meet you.

5 ⊙72 Listen to the conversations. Check your answers.

6 Work in pairs. Practise the conversations, changing roles.

Role-play

7 Work in pairs. Role-play some conversations with a partner.

Learner A: Look at the role cards on page 123 and follow the instructions.
Learner B: Look at the role cards on page 126 and follow the instructions.

Formal introductions

8 Practise introducing yourself to an audience. Use the phrases from the Language Support box below.

Good morning/afternoon/evening, dear colleagues. My name is Igor Petrov. I'm an Associate Professor at Moscow State University, Russia. I'm honoured to be here.

⊙73 **Language Support: introductions at a conference**

Introducing yourself	**Introducing other people**
I'm honoured to be here.	I am happy to introduce our guest to you.
It's a pleasure to be here.	It is an honour to introduce our colleague from …
I'm glad to be here again.	I'd like to introduce … He/She is our guest speaker from …

---

9 Imagine your partner is a guest speaker at your university. Introduce him/her to the class. Use phrases from the Language Support box.

I'd like to welcome Sam Dines, Marketing Director of ABC Company. Some of you met him last year at the autumn conference. He's a very well-known expert on world financial markets and the author of several textbooks we recommend to our students. It's good to have you here again, Sam.

Lesson 2 Starting and keeping a conversation going

Lead-in

1 Work in pairs and discuss this question. What is necessary to keep a conversation going?

2 Read the conversation below. Then write the correct verb at the end of each line to explain the purpose of the sentence. You will use one verb twice.

> Add   Answer   Ask

A: Who do you work for? **1**_____
B: I work for Arcada University of Applied Sciences. **2**_____
   I am with the Business, Information Technology and Media Department. **3**_____
   And what about you? Who do you work for? **4**_____

3 Work out the '3As' rule of successful communication.

> A_ _ + A_ _ _ _ _ + A_ _ = success

Asking questions

> **Tip:**
>
> The first five minutes of a conversation with someone you don't know can be rather difficult. The best way to get a conversation going is to ask questions. Start with a question about the other person rather than a statement about yourself. An easy way to keep the conversation going is to ask: *And what about you?*

4 Complete these questions. You will need to use different verb forms (e.g. Present Simple, Past Simple, etc.).

1 Who / work for?   *Who do you work for?*
2 Which part / country / come from?
3 first time / in Brazil?
4 know / many people here?
5 How / enjoying / the conference?
6 How / get / here?
7 Where / staying?
8 often / go to / international conferences?

5 Work in pairs. Role-play the questions in Activity 4, using the '3As' rule of successful communication.

Follow-up questions

Tip:

We often ask follow-up questions to develop a conversation. Many of these follow-up questions begin with the question word *How*.

A: How is the coffee?
B: Just how I like it – sweet and hot.

---

6 Make questions from these prompts.

1 How / day?
2 How / flight?
3 How / conference?
4 How / new boss?
5 How / presentation?
6 How / audience?
7 How / hotel?
8 How / meeting?
9 How / training course?
10 How / the weather?
11 How / dessert?
12 How / new job?

7 Work in pairs. Follow these steps.

1 Learner A: Ask your partner questions 1–6 from Activity 6.
2 Learner B: Answer the questions, choosing an appropriate response from the list on your card page 126.
3 Learner B: Ask your partner questions 7–12 from Activity 6.
4 Learner A: Answer the questions, choosing an appropriate response from the list on your card page 123.

Role-play

8 Work in pairs. Role-play some conversations. Use the '3As' rule of communication and *How*-questions.

Learner A: look at page 123 and follow the instructions.
Learner B: look at page 126 and follow the instructions.

Lesson 3 Showing interest and reacting to news

Lead-in

1 Complete the diagram with examples a–e. The first has been done for you.

a Is she?
b Do they have a date for it yet?
c Wow, that's fantastic!
d ~~My daughter's getting married~~.
e Yes, three weeks from now. It's my birthday!

A: Give a piece of news.
e.g. ¹ *My daughter is getting married.*

B: Echo the question.
e.g. ² _____ .

B: React / Give a personal response.
e.g. ³ _____ .

A: Respond with more information.
e.g. ⁵ _____ .

B: Ask a follow-up question.
e.g. ⁴ _____ .

2 Work in pairs. Read the pieces of news below. Think of possible echo-questions, responses and follow-up questions. Use phrases from the Language Support box.

1 A: I couldn't sleep last night.
　B: *Couldn't you? That's a pity. Why?*
　A: There was a very noisy party downstairs.
2 A: I've received a scholarship from the Erasmus Programme.
　B: _____
　A: To Austria.
3 A: We couldn't find Mike last night.
　B: _____
　A: He said he met his old university friend and they ended up in one of the cafés.
4 A: It was the best holiday we've ever had.
　B: _____
　A: We rented a car and travelled all around the country.
5 A: There's going to be a prize-giving ceremony at the end of the conference.
　B: _____ .
　A: Because I have a lot of contacts.

⊙74 **Language Support: showing interest**

Reacting to good news
How nice! / Great!
Wow, that's fantastic!
Lucky you. I wish I was going!
Congratulations – you must be delighted!

Reacting to bad news
How awful! / Poor you!
What a pity! / That's too bad.

Reacting with surprise
You're joking. / You're kidding.
No! That's strange!
Really?
What? You don't say!

Active listening

3 Read conversations 1 and 2 below and complete the sentences with phrases from the boxes. Sometimes, more than one answer may be correct.

Conversation 1: two people are waiting to get on a plane.

> Yeah   Is it?   Yes   I see.   Really?
> What a coincidence!   Right.   That's great!   That would be great.

Zbignev: It looks like we're going to be here a while, huh?

Helga: ¹_____ I'm getting used to these delays.

Zbignev: Do you travel a lot?

Helga: Quite a lot, yes. It's part of my job.

Zbignev: ²_____ And what do you do?

Helga: I'm the Assistant Director of the Center for International Programmes in New Mexico State University. Helga Romirez, and you?

Zbignev: I'm Zbignev Kozlovsky, from Gdansk. Nice to meet you, Helga.

Helga: Nice to meet you too. Have you ever been to Rotterdam?

Zbignev: ³_____ , this is my second visit. I'm staying with the Erasmus University for a month to carry out some research.

Helga: ⁴_____ I'm going to the University as well. I've been invited to participate in the International Education Exhibition. I have to present our Center.

Zbignev: ⁵_____ How long are you going to stay?

Helga: A week.

Zbignev: Would you like to meet one day? I can show you around the city.

Helga: ⁶_____ Oh, our plane is boarding.

Conversation 2: at a conference dinner, a woman is placed next to a man she doesn't know. He is trying to make a conversation with her but some of his questions annoy her.

> Well   By the way   That's right.   Uhm.
> That's something I'd love to discuss with you

Man: So, how do you know Justin?

Woman: We worked on the project two years ago in Tomsk.

Man: Aha, you must be a teacher from Russia.

Woman: ¹_____ .

Man: And what does your husband do?

Woman: ²_____ , I'm divorced.

Man: Oh, sorry. Anyway, so tell me, why do you, Russians, celebrate two New Years? Does it have any religious implications?

Woman: ³_____ , it's just an excuse to have a longer public holiday.

Man: Hmm, interesting. ⁴_____ , what do you think about your new prime minister?

Woman: ⁵_____ , but can we do it at another time?

4 Work in pairs. Compare your answers to Activity 3 with a partner. What is the purpose of the phrases in the boxes?

5 Work in pairs. Practise the conversations.

Lesson 4 Inviting

Lead-in

1 There is going to be an international conference at your university. You have been asked to organise entertainment for visitors. Look at the list of things for visitors to do. Which can you do where you live? What other things can you add?

- go bowling
- go to the theatre
- have a barbecue party
- visit a historical site

Inviting

2 Read the phrases in the Language Support box and put them in three groups.

a Inviting
b Accepting invitations
c Declining invitations

⊙75 **Language Support: invitations**

Why don't you join us for a cup of coffee? *Inviting*
Thank you. That'd be a pleasure.
I'd like to, but I'm afraid …
Thanks but I can't make it then.
That's very kind of you, but I don't think I can.
Would you like to join me for dinner?
Thank you very much. That would be very nice.
Would you be interested in going to see an exhibition?
Thank you for inviting me. I'll look forward to it.
How about / What about going to the theatre tonight?
That's very kind of you. I'd love to come.
Would you like to visit the museum?
That would be nice, but unfortunately ….
Thanks. That sounds great / like fun.

---

3 ⊙75 Listen and check your answers.

4 Listen again and repeat the phrases.

5 Work in pairs. Imagine that you are talking in the coffee break during the conference.

Learner A: Invite a colleague to one of the social events from Activity 1.
Learner B: Your colleague is inviting you to some social events. Accept or reject the invitations.

A: Would you like to go bowling tonight?
B: Thanks. That sounds fun. / I'd like to, but I have other plans for the evening.

Accepting or declining

6 Work in pairs. Sentences 1–12 come from two conversations. Put the sentences in each conversation in order. The first sentence of each conversation has been done for you.

Conversation 1: Accepting an invitation	Conversation 2: Declining an invitation
2 I don't know what your plans are, but would you like to go out for dinner tomorrow?	*7 Look, it's a bit chilly outside. How about having a cup of tea here?*

1 Fine. About what time?
2 ~~I don't know what your plans are, but would you like to go out for dinner tomorrow?~~
3 Great.
4 Shall I pick you up at the hotel?
5 Don't mention it. It was my pleasure.
6 Is 7 o'clock OK?
7 ~~Look, it's a bit chilly outside. How about having a cup of tea here?~~
8 That's a pity. Have a safe flight then.
9 Thanks. I'd love to. Where shall we meet?
10 Thank you very much for everything. I really appreciate it.
11 I'd love to, but I need an early night. My flight is at 6 tomorrow morning.
12 See you tomorrow at 7, then.

7 ⊙76 **Listen to the conversations. Check your answers.**

8 Work in pairs. Practise the conversations.

Saying 'no'

> **Tip:**
> If you cannot accept an invitation, it is polite to apologise and/or thank the person and then give reasons.

9 Work in pairs. Read the reasons for declining invitations. Think of possible invitations and ways of saying 'no' in each situation. Use phrases from the Language Support box.

1 A: *How about going to the cinema tonight? Would you like to join us?*
  B: *No, thanks.* I'm a bit tired. It has been a long day.
2 A: _____
  B: _____ I've already made plans for tonight.
3 A: _____
  B: _____ I already have other plans. Another time maybe.
4 A: _____
  B: _____ I'm quite busy on Monday.
5 A: _____
  B: _____ I still have some work to do.
6 A: _____
  B: _____ I need an early night. My flight is at six tomorrow morning.
7 A: _____
  B: _____ I won't be here at the weekend.

10 Work in pairs. Practise the conversations.

Role-play

11 Work in pairs. Role-play some conversations.

Learner A: Look at page 123 and follow the instructions.
Learner B: Look at page 126 and follow the instructions.

Lesson 5 Paying and receiving compliments

Lead-in

1 Is it appropriate to pay compliments in your culture?

2 Work in groups. Think of situations in which you usually pay compliments.

Complimenting

A   B   C   D

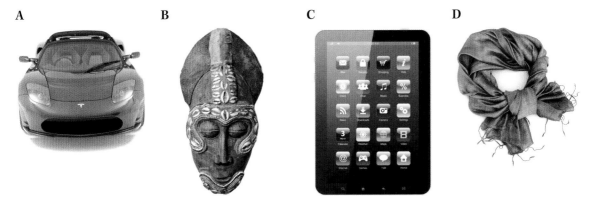

3 ⊙77 Listen to five speakers giving compliments. Match the compliments to the photos. (One of the compliments can be used for two photos, and one for all four photos.)

Being nice

> ⊙78 **Language Support: complimenting**
>
> **Paying compliments**
> What a wonderful picture/house/party!
> Good/Nice job. Congratulations!
> You've done a really good job. Congratulations! (informal)
> You were terrific. (informal)
> Your slides/presentation were/was fantastic/terrific! (informal)
> I thought you/your students were brilliant. Congratulations! (informal)
>
> **Responding to compliments**
> Do you really think so? Thanks.
> I'm glad you liked it.
> Thank you very much.
> It wasn't difficult at all.
> How nice of you to say so/that!
> In fact, the credit should also go to my colleagues. (formal)
> It was nothing special, really.

4 Work in pairs. Complete the conversations below. Use phrases from the Language Support box to help you.

1 At your colleague's birthday party:
   A: What a delicious cake you've made!
   B: _____
   A: You're a wonderful cook! Everything tastes so good.
   B: _____

2 After a presentation:
   A: _____
   B: In fact, the credit should also go to my assistant. She is so good at preparing slideshows.
   A: Did she use some special software?
   B: I'm not sure. You'd better ask her.

3 In your friend's new office:
   A: What a nice office you have!
   B: _____
   A: This photo of the sunset looks fantastic!
   B: _____ . A friend of mine sent it to me from Oregon.

4 After a students' conference:
   A: I thought your students were brilliant.
   B: _____
   A: Their English is very good. To talk about finance must be very difficult even in your own language.
   B: You're right, but they are very motivated and work hard.

5 On the last day of the conference:
   A: I just wanted to say: you have organised an excellent conference.
   _____ . Your team worked so well together.
   B: _____

5 Work in pairs. Practise the conversations.

Role-play

6 Work in pairs. Role-play some conversations with a partner. Use the '3As' rule of successful communication.

Learner A: Look at page 124 and follow the instructions.
Learner B: Look at page 127 and follow the instructions.

Lesson 6 Saying thank you, sorry and goodbye

Lead-in

1 **Work in groups. Discuss the questions.**

1 Is it polite to leave a place without saying goodbye?
2 How do you usually say goodbye in your culture?

2 **List some English phrases you know that are used at the end of informal conversations, at public events (e.g. after conferences) or formal meetings.**

Finishing a conversation

3 **Read the conversations and decide which is more formal. How do you know?**

Conversation 1
A: Mr Borisov, the department head of my university is starting a new project. I am wondering if you are interested in participating.
B: Well, Mr Allan, do you mean something similar to what I did for your department last year?
A: No, the whole concept is totally different.
B: Oh, it sounds interesting. Do you think you can describe the idea behind it briefly?
A: No, I don't think so. I suggest that we go to the conference room and have a look at some PDF files.
B: Will you excuse me? I'm afraid I must go now as I have tickets for a concert tonight. Could we do it tomorrow?
A: Oh, yes, I see. I'm sorry. Enjoy the concert, Mr Borisov, and I look forward to seeing you tomorrow.
B: Thank you, Mr Allan. It was nice talking to you. Goodbye.
A: Bye.

Conversation 2
A: Hi, Bryan. I've downloaded some excellent pictures. Want to have a look?
B: What kind of pictures are they?
A: My family holiday in Paphos, Cyprus.
B: Oh, Cyprus. Sounds interesting! I'm thinking about going there, too.
A: It's a great place! Let's go to my room, and I'll show you the photos.
B: Oh, sorry, Andy, but I can't make it right now. I have tickets for a concert tonight. Can we meet tomorrow?
A: Sure, how about after lunch?
B: Great.
A: Enjoy the concert, see you tomorrow.
B: Thanks. See you.

4 **Read the conversations again and find pairs of formal/informal phrases used to do the following.**

a say goodbye
b apologise
c show understanding of what has been said
d thank someone.

5 **Work in pairs and compare your list of phrases.**

6 **Work in pairs. Practise the conversations.**

Role-play

7 Learner A, look at page 124. Learner B, look on page 127. Do the tasks below.

1 Decide whether the conversation needs to be formal or informal.
2 Role-play the conversation with a partner, using phrases from the Language Support box.

⊙ 79 **Language Support: saying thank you, sorry and goodbye**

Formal
I've enjoyed talking to you, but I'm afraid I must go now.
Will you excuse me? Unfortunately, I have to go now.
It was really enjoyable.
It's been nice talking to you.
I look forward to seeing you again.
It has been nice meeting you, Ms Zaretsky. Goodbye.
See you again soon, I hope. Please get in touch.
I'm afraid I really must be on my way.

Informal
Thanks for everything.
It's a pleasure to meet/see you.
Sorry, have to leave now.
Sorry, but I'd better get going. I'll give you a call/email you.
Bye, take care.
See you soon.
See you around.
Have a good trip back.

Follow-up

8 You are going to talk to your partner for at least three minutes. To prepare for the conversation, do the tasks below.

1 Read the situation and the beginning of a conversation.

Imagine that you're stuck in a lift with someone you don't know. You know that repairs are in progress, and you have to be patient. To pass the time, you talk to the person who is next to you.

A: I hope they repair it soon.
B: Well, the only thing to do now is to wait. By the way, my name is …

---

2 Decide on your name, country, occupation, hobby, etc.
3 Work with your partner and plan the stages of the conversation (e.g. introducing yourselves to each other, talking about where you come from, your job, etc.).
4 Decide on the phrases you need for each stage of the conversation (see the Language Support boxes in Lessons 1–6).
5 Make notes, if necessary.
6 Practise the conversation. Decide what can be improved.
7 Role-play the conversation.

Unit 2 Presentation skills

By the end of this unit you will be able to

➡ identify your strengths and weaknesses as a presenter

➡ use a stock of phrases for presentations

➡ use visuals effectively

➡ plan, structure and give a clear, effective final 10-minute presentation in English

Lesson 1 What makes a good presentation?

Lead-in

1 Work in pairs. Read the quotation below and discuss the questions.

1 Do you agree with the quotation? Why/Why not?
2 Who does it seem relevant to?

A man who cannot speak well will never make a career. (Anonymous)

Successful presentations

2 Work in groups. Think of a good lecture or presentation you have seen. What was it about? Why was it successful?

3 Work in groups. Make a list of what makes a successful lecture/presentation.

The speaker was confident.

4 Make a spidergram of your ideas from Activity 3.

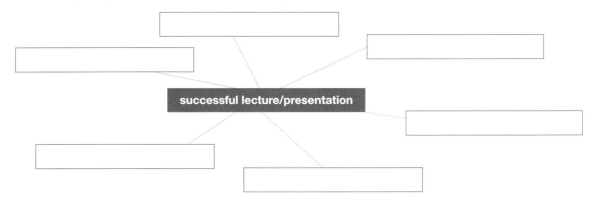

successful lecture/presentation

5 Compare your spidergram with other groups. Are your ideas similar or different?

> **Tip:**
> You can use online tools for creating a spidergram.

Questionnaire: reflect on your experience

6 Think of a presentation you have given recently. Complete the questionnaire below. Write *yes* or *no* next to each question.

> **Did you:**
> 1 prepare thoroughly: check the meaning and pronunciation of new words, create slides, rehearse the speech, etc.?
> 2 start the talk in an interesting way to get the attention of the audience?
> 3 speak from notes rather than read a whole text?
> 4 give an overview of your talk at the beginning?
> 5 use phrases to help the audience follow your ideas?
> 6 provide examples to illustrate complex and/or original ideas?
> 7 provide visual support?
> 8 invite the audience to ask questions?
> 9 emphasise the main points by slowing down and leaving pauses?
> 10 make eye contact with your audience?
> 11 avoid repetitive use of 'pet' words or phrases (e.g. *so, well, OK, like*)?
> 12 use effective gestures?

7 How many positive answers have you got? What would you like to improve?

My goal is to get rid of phrases like 'well' which I use too often.

The audience

> **Tip:**
> When we give a presentation, we speak to the audience. The presenter should make the information interesting and useful for them.

8 Work in groups. Think of conferences where you were sitting in the audience. Say what you don't like about some presenters' behaviour.

What I really hate is when a presenter just reads what's on the slides.

9 What should a presenter know about the audience in order to meet their expectations? Make a list and compare it with other people in the group.

The presenter should know what the audience knows.

Presentation criteria

10 Work in groups. Make a list of criteria for evaluating a presentation. Take into account the ideas you discussed in this lesson. Present your criteria to the group.

Presentation goal

> **Tip:**
> The structure, style, and delivery of a presentation depend on its goals. There are normally several goals, but it is possible to choose a primary one.

11 Match events 1–8, which involve speaking in public, to definitions a–h.

1 lecture
2 briefing
3 demonstration
4 seminar
5 workshop
6 press conference
7 conference presentation
8 commercial presentation

a a formal talk on a serious subject given to a group of people, especially students
b an occasion when a teacher or expert and a group of people meet to study and discuss something
c a meeting of people to discuss and/or perform practical work in a subject or activity
d a talk describing a product that can be bought
e a talk to people of the same field, usually about your research
f the act of showing someone how to do something, or how something works
g a meeting where information is given to someone just before they do something
h a meeting at which a person or organisation makes a public statement and reporters can ask questions

12 What kind of talks have you given? Who was your audience?

13 Read the phrases from the Language Support box. Work in groups. Discuss which goals (from the box) are suitable for the presentation types given in Activity 11. There may be more than one possible answer.

Language Support: presentation goals

to inspire people to act
to persuade, to gain agreement
to teach or to pass on information
to explore or debate ideas

to entertain
to report on the results of projects/research
to sell, promote something
to share ideas

I think [goal] is possible because ...
The aim of [presentation type] is to ...

Presentation structure

14 Put the stages of a presentation (a–l) in a logical order. Different answers are possible.

a present the main body of the talk
b handle questions
c signal the beginning of the talk
d greet the audience
e summarise the main points
f introduce yourself
g have a strong ending

h introduce the presentation topic and objectives
i outline the presentation structure
j thank the audience
k thank the organisers
l say when you would like to take questions

15 Work in pairs and compare your order. Discuss the reasons for any differences. Use the phrases from the Language Support box below.

Language Support: opinions

In my opinion, ... (formal)
In my view, ... (formal)

Personally, I think/believe that...
I guess ... (informal)

---

16 Work in groups. How is the structure of a lecture different from the structure of a conference presentation?

Starting a presentation

17 Look at the phrases below. Do they introduce a topic (T), introduce the plan of your presentation (P), set goals (G), or deal with questions (Q)?

1 What I'd like to do is to discuss … _____
2 If you have any questions, please feel free to interrupt. _____
3 The aim of my presentation is … _____
4 I'm going to deal with three aspects of the subject …, first … _____
5 What I intend to do is to explain … _____
6 My topic today is … _____
7 Today, I'm going to talk about … _____
8 I've divided my presentation into three sections. _____
9 I'll be happy to answer questions at the end. _____

18 ⊙ 80 Listen and check your answers.

> **Tip:**
> Memorise the phrases. This will help you to sound confident.

Follow-up

19 You are going to give a short talk to the class about an event in your field. Your goal is to inform your colleagues about the coming event and encourage them to take part in it. Do the tasks below.

1 Search online for an online course/webinar in your field of study.
2 Choose an event that you would like to participate in. Make notes, using the questions below to help you.
 a What is the topic?
 b When is the course/webinar?
 c Who is giving the course/webinar?
 d What should you do to take part in it?
 e Why should people in your field take this course or join this webinar?
3 Use your notes to plan a three-minute briefing in English. Use the phrases from Activities 13 and 17 to explain the goal of your talk and when you would like to take questions.
4 Choose phrases from the Language Support box below to make recommendations.
5 Practise your talk. (If possible, record your voice digitally.)
6 Think of ways to improve your talk.
7 Take turns to give your three-minute briefing to the class, using your notes.

> **Language Support: advice and recommendations**
>
> It may be worth (+ verb + -*ing*)   You should (+ verb)
> How about (+ verb + -*ing*)?   Perhaps you could (+ verb)

Lesson 2 Developing presentation skills

Lead-in

1 ⊙81 Look at the phrases in the Language Support box and put them in two groups: Agreeing and Disagreeing. Then listen and check.

⊙81 **Language Support: agreement and disagreement**

I fully agree with you / this statement.
Absolutely!
I'm afraid I can't agree with ..., I'm afraid.
I think so, too.

I don't see it quite like that.
That's (very) true.
I'm not sure I quite agree that...

---

2 Work in groups. Discuss what makes a stronger impact on the audience: <u>what</u> the presenter says or <u>how</u> he/she says it. Use the phrases in Activity 1.

Titles

3 Work in groups. Read these titles for presentations on using technology in teaching. Choose the one(s) you think is (are) best. Give reasons.

1 How to Teach with ICT at University
2 New Classroom Research Reveals the ICT Teaching Methodology that Gets the Best Results
3 How to Teach with ICT and Make Students Think
4 How to Be an Inspiring ICT Teacher
5 The #1 Strategy for Teaching with ICT

Lecture on study skills

4 Look quickly at two parts of a lecture on study skills. Answer the questions.

1 What is the topic of each part?
2 What advice does the lecturer give to students? Do you agree? Why/Why not?

Once you have chosen a topic   The second step   While getting ready
The first point   First of all   Then   At this stage   After that

---

Well, let's start, shall we? **1**_____ I'd like to make is that thorough preparation is a foundation for a successful presentation or a lecture. **2**_____ , carry out research into it. Find out as much as you can about the topic; use in-house material, websites, journals, and make the topic of your presentation more specific. My recommendation is to address some significant issue in the area you researched into. The topic should make an impact scientifically, socially, educationally, and so on. Just a report on your or somebody else's achievements is not very interesting. Think about what might be interesting to your audience. Ask yourself questions: Why am I giving this presentation? What do I want the audience to gain? What do they already know about the topic? **3**_____ , gather as many facts as you can, take notes, carefully indicating the source and the author in case you decide to borrow somebody's ideas or quote their research results. You will need them later to put the references on slides.

4_____ in preparation is to properly structure the information you have collected, so that the audience can easily follow your ideas. **5**_____ , you should again narrow the topic down to make it manageable within the time given.

You cannot share everything you know about the subject within 15 minutes, can you?
6_____ , from your notes, choose no more than three major points you're
going to focus on during the presentation. 7_____ , think of how you're going
to develop these ideas: through examples and explanations, statistics and facts, or/and
referring to an authority or your own research results, etc. 8_____ , you can
create a spidergram of the ideas you want to express in a note form and/or make a list of the
most important ones and then put them in a logical order. Now with this plan in mind, you're
ready to write the text itself. My advice is to start with the body, not the introduction.

Firstly   One more popular method for   Secondly   Thirdly   Another way to
As for text organisation   For example   we can now move to the last point of
That is why   And the last piece of advice for today

What makes a presentation powerful? Clarity. What makes it clear? Logic and language. A clear
text is logically constructed, with all the parts linked together, and with enough signals for the
listeners to follow the ideas of the speaker. The text should be simple enough to understand
and the language should be expressive enough to impress the audience. If you can keep this in
mind, you're on the right path to success.

9_____ , there are several typical ways depending on the purpose of the
presentation and the content you're going to deliver. 10_____ , you can present
information chronologically if the purpose of the presentation is to show a historical dimension of a
phenomenon or a sequence of steps in a process. 11_____ ,
your presentation can follow a problem–solution pattern if you are after finding effective ways
to deal with a certain obstacle or hurdle. 12_____ , you can compose your
text using a cause-effect relationship between the phenomena or events you're talking about.
13_____ organise the text is to adhere to a topical approach, when the
presentation is divided into subtopics relevant to the subject of the talk in order to give a broad
picture of the area. 14_____ organising ideas (especially for presentations that aim
to describe a situation) is the use of Wh-questions: *who, what, where, when, how, which* is often
called a journalistic approach. The discourse markers that signpost the progression of your ideas
depend on the type of text organisation. 15_____ , the cause-effect relationship is
signalled with the help of such phrases as *this leads to, it resulted in/from, this affected, due to*.

Mentioning discourse markers, 16_____ my lecture today, which is the power
of language. I'd like to quote Ralph Waldo Emerson: 'Words are also actions, and actions
are a kind of words.' It is true! The impact of your presentation depends entirely on you, your
text, your content, your words. 17_____ you should choose the words wisely
and carefully; empowering words lead to powerful results! Create a picture in the mind of the
listeners: use comparisons and metaphors, dramatic contrasts and emphasis. Do not overdo
specific terminology or abbreviations - they may be not known to the audience. Use a simple,
short sentence structure with active verbs rather than passive. Show who the author is; do not
hide behind passive constructions.

18_____ ... Make sure you know the meaning, usage and pronunciation of
every word you use in English. If necessary, consult a monolingual dictionary. You'd better
not heavily rely on electronic translators like Google Translate or Multitran; they are useful for
phrases and expressions, not complete sentences or paragraphs.

---

5 Read the lecture and complete it with the phrases from the lists. Sometimes, more
than one answer may be possible.

6 Give the lecture a title. Then compare your ideas in pairs and choose the best one.

A good start

> **Tip:**
> The first three minutes of a presentation are key to its success. You need to get the attention of the audience.

7 Match the ways of starting a presentation (1–7) to examples (a–g) of those ways.

1 a personal story
2 an amazing fact or statistic
3 a quotation
4 involving the audience
5 a rhetorical question
6 a joke
7 an overview of the situation

a Do you know that fear of speaking in front of an audience comes second after the fear of death? That's why I decided to prepare a presentation aiming at …

b Before we start, could you raise your hands if you have to give presentations quite often? Oh, I see there is a lot of expertise in the room. Let's share it.

c I'd like to begin today's presentation with a quote by Woodrow Wilson 'If I am to speak ten minutes, I need a week for preparation; if fifteen minutes, three days; if half an hour, two days; if an hour, I am ready now.' It took me years to be able to speak well in public and I'd like to share …

d When I started my teaching career, my first lecture was a real disaster. I wasn't able to take off my eyes from the notes and read the whole lecture without looking at the students. They were bored! I decided to improve my presentation skills. That's how I finally came to lecturing on speaking in public.

e Nowadays, very many books on developing presentation skills and courses are available, both for face-to-face and online practice in speaking. They contain tips and recommendations; however … .

f Once a teacher asked, 'What do you call a person who keeps on talking when people are no longer interested?' And the pupil's answer was: 'A teacher.' A joke or the truth? Today we're going to discuss what makes the audience engaged.

g Why do we know best how to make a presentation when it concerns others, but when it's about ourselves we sometimes fail to get our message across at a conference?

8 Work in groups. Discuss these ways of starting a presentation. Say whether they are essential, helpful or unhelpful for your personal presentation style.

I think that a joke is unhelpful for my presentation style as I can't tell jokes.

Beginning your presentation

9 At the end of this unit, you're going to deliver a 10-minute presentation or lecture. Think of the topic. To practise the beginning, do the tasks below.

1 Give your presentation a name.
2 Think of three main points to include in your presentation. Write a plan.
3 Revise the structure of a presentation and phrases to introduce yourself, the topic, purpose, and plan.
4 Think of how to start your presentation strongly.
5 Practise a one-minute beginning for your presentation.

10 Work in groups. Present the beginning of your presentation to the group, using your notes.

> **Tip:**
> Do not apologise if you think that you are not very good at presenting. If you decide to present, the audience assumes that you will be prepared.

11 Work in groups. Listen to each other's presentation beginnings. Provide feedback, using the following questions as guidelines.

1 Did the presenters greet the audience?
2 Did they introduce themselves, the topic and the plan?
3 Did they mention the time and when they wanted to take questions?
4 Did they use a technique for starting a presentation?
5 Was the beginning clear?
6 Did the presenters look confident?

Supporting your ideas

> **Tip:**
> While making a presentation, you need to support your ideas. The general rule for idea development is: statement of your idea → explanation/clarification → example/illustration.

12 Read the card the teacher will give you. There are two statements on the same topic. Choose one statement that you'd like to develop.

13 Look at the Language Support box below and choose phrases that can help you to support the statement on the card.

> **Language Support: supporting ideas ...**
>
> **... with factual information**
> The statistics show that ...
> It is a well-known fact that ...
> Actually / in fact ...
> To illustrate this with, I can provide some numbers/facts.
>
> **... comparing/contrasting**
> Let's compare it with ...
> In contrast to X, Y ...
> It is the same as ...
>
> **... with evidence**
> According to ...
> With reference to...
> X claims that ...
> X is in favour of/against ...
>
> **... with a description**
> This process involves such steps as ...
> The conditions in which ...
> X is shaped as ...
> It is integral to ...

14 Prepare a one-minute presentation to develop the statement you have chosen. Make notes.

15 Work in groups. Take turns to give your one-minute presentation. After each presentation give feedback to the presenter.

Your mini-talk

16 You are going to give a three-minute presentation. To get ready, do the tasks below.

1 Choose one of the following options.

   a Imagine that you are talking at the meeting of your research board, making a case for continued funding for your research. Talk about your research.

   b Imagine that you are talking to foreign guests who have come to visit your university. You give them information necessary for a collaborative project between the institutions. Prepare a mini-presentation about your university.

   c Practise a short presentation of your own choice or continue the one you started in Activity 9.

2 Think of what you can include in your presentation. Write a plan.

3 Prepare language you need and make notes.

4 Write the text of your presentation. To structure your presentation, use phrases from the Language Support box below.

Language Support: signposting

Ordering points
There are two kinds of theories / two steps involved. The first is ... The second is ...
Firstly, / Secondly, / Thirdly,
Next, Then, Lastly, Finally, ...

Moving on
I'd like now to move on to ...
Turning now to...
The next point is ...
Another interesting point is ...

Giving examples
For example, ...
For instance, ...

Putting it in other words
The point I'm making is ...
What I'm suggesting is ...

Emphasising
Furthermore, ...
This supports my argument that ...

---

5 Practise your presentation. Record yourself digitally if possible.

17 Take turns to give your presentation in class. Listen to your colleagues' presentations and make notes in the table below. You will need these notes later.

Presenter's name	Topic	Main points
		1
		2
		3

18 Ask questions after each presentation. For questions and answers, use phrases from the Language Support box below.

⊙ 82 **Language Support: Questions and answers – techniques**

Getting more information
Could I ask you a couple of questions, please?
Could you tell me some more about ...?
Excuse me, do you know ...?

Before answering a question
Thank you, that's a very interesting question.
I'm glad you asked that question.
I'm not sure, let me check.

Dealing with difficult questions
We don't have enough evidence to show that ...
I'd prefer to deal with that point later.
Maybe we could discuss that in more detail after the session.

Ending a question and answer session
If there are no (more) questions, we'll finish there.
We only have time for one more question, please.
I'm afraid, that's all the time we have. Thank you.

Concluding a presentation

19 Work in groups. You are going to prepare a one-minute conclusion for one of your colleagues' presentations. Do the tasks below.

1 Decide whose presentation you are going to write a conclusion for.

Tip:
In a conclusion, the presenter usually summarises the main points of his/her presentation, provides recommendations, or future directions and steps. It does not contain new information. Another function of the conclusion is to leave an impression, to finish strongly.

2 Look at the notes you made in Activity 17. Write a summary of the main points.
3 Read the phrases from the Language Support box below. Choose one to use in your conclusion.

Language Support: closing a presentation
First we looked at ... and we saw that ...
Then we considered ... and I argued that ...
In conclusion, I'd like to emphasise that ...
To sum up, there are two conclusions/recommendations ...
That completes my presentation. Thank you.

4 Present your conclusion to the group.

20 Work in the same groups. Listen to all the conclusions. Provide feedback, using the following questions as guidelines. The author of the presentation should start first.

1 Was it an accurate summary of the main points?
2 Was the conclusion signalled?
3 Was it strong?

Lesson 3 Working with visuals

Lead-in

1 Work in groups. Think about presentations you have seen at conferences. Create a list of *dos* and *don'ts* for an effective slide-based presentation. Use phrases from the Language Support boxes on opinions on page 109 and agreement and disagreement on page 111 to help you express opinions and agree or disagree with each other.

Do	Don't
• give a title to each slide	• use complete sentences

Information exchange

2 Work in pairs. Exchange information about a presentation slide.

1 Learner A, go to page 125. Learner B, go to page 128. Read through the sentences and underline the verb in each sentence.
2 Think of a question to complete each gap in your text.
   A: What does the first slide usually contain?
   B: What does the second slide show?
3 Take turns to ask each other questions and fill in the gaps.
4 In pairs, compare your texts to check the information you have filled in. What information is new to you?

Improving slides

3 Go to page 129 and read the *Slides Checklist*. Match the words and phrases (1–4) below from the checklist to their definitions (a–d).

1 outline slide
2 prompt
3 conclusion slide
4 background

a a point on a slide that you use in your presentation – it can be a word, a figure or a short phrase
b the part at the back of a slide, not the main words and pictures the viewer looks at
c a slide containing a general plan of what you are going to present
d a slide summarising the key points of your presentation

A

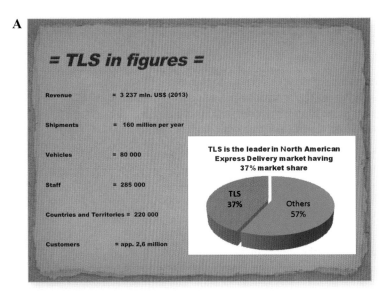

B

C

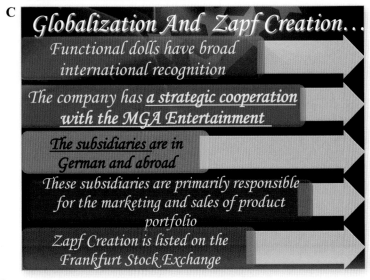

4 Work in pairs. Look at slides A–C on page 118. How can the slides be improved? Use the *Slides Checklist* to guide you. Use phrases from the Language Support boxes on opinions on page 109 and agreement and disagreement on page 111 to help your discussion.

In my opinion, there is too much information on one slide. It is worth having three slides.

> **Tip:**
> If you have several slides related to the same topic, repeat the heading on each slide. You may also need to number the slides in case the audience would like you to go back to a certain slide.

Creating slides

5 Plan a five-minute presentation with the use of slides. Choose from the options below.

1 A short presentation on a subject of your choice.
2 The beginning of your final presentation.

6 Make a maximum of five slides to support your presentation. Include the name of your presentation, an overview of the presentation, at least one main-body slide, and a conclusion slide.

> **Tip:**
> One of the most typical mistakes many presenters make is to put too many words on a slide. Use key words. Do not read the text from the slides, talk to the audience.

7 Work in pairs. Exchange your slides and provide feedback, using the *Slides Checklist* from Activity 3.

Presenting statistics

8 Work in groups. Discuss the questions.

1 How much statistical data do you typically have to present?
2 What type of visual support do you use if you need to present the data?
3 What difficulties do you experience when describing graphs?

9 ⊙ 83 Listen and repeat the numbers in the table.

200	100	60,000	20,000
80%	¼	50,000	1,000
17	300,000,000	170	43

10 Work in pairs. Complete the facts below about the human body, using the numbers from Activity 9.

Some interesting facts about the human body

1 Nerve impulses to and from the brain travel as fast as _____ miles per hour.

2 The human brain cell can hold five times as much information as the *Encyclopedia Britannica*. The storage capacity of the brain in electronic terms is between three or even _____ terabytes.

3 _____ of the brain is water.

4 The human body has _____ miles of blood vessels.

5 Sneezes regularly exceed _____ miles per hour.

6 Your nose can remember _____ different scents.

7 It takes _____ muscles to smile and _____ to frown.

8 You use _____ muscles to take one step.

9 Bone has been found to have a tensile strength of _____ pounds per square inch (psi) while steel is much higher at 70,000 psi.

10 The feet account for _____ of all the human body's bones.

11 _____ cells die in the human body every minute.

Follow-up

11 Write down six or seven examples of numerical data you often use. Work in pairs and swap your numbers. Practise pronouncing your partner's numbers.

12 Make a slide with a diagram which is relevant to your specialism. Show it to the class.

13 Work in pairs and swap your diagrams. Try to describe your partner's visual. Use phrases from the Language Support box below.

⊙84 **Language Support: referring to visuals**

If you look at the figure, …
As you can see, the figure shows/gives …
As the figure/diagram shows, …
As can be seen, …
Look at this flowchart/diagram.
The horizontal axis represents …
The table/diagram summarises the data …
As the line graph/diagram shows, there was an upward trend in …

---

14 Comment on your partner's interpretation of your slide. Is it accurate?

15 Give feedback on the quality of your partner's diagram (e.g. size, complexity, layout). Use phrases from the Language Support boxes on opinions on page 109 and agreement and disagreement on page 111 to help your discussion.

Lesson 4 Your presentation skills

Lead-in

1 Look again at the questionnaire in Lesson 1, Activity 6 on page 108 and do it again.

2 Are the answers different? Do you have more positive answers than before? What do you need to improve, in your opinion?

Academic culture checklist

3 Read the checklist and tick the statements that are true for presentations in your field of study.

Structure	
Presentations are very logical, developing the main idea step by step.	☐
Presentations are digressive with many deviations from the main subject.	☐

Language and content	
The language of presentations is informal.	☐
The language of presentations is formal.	☐
Presentations contain detailed information, with lots of supporting data and examples.	☐
Presentations contain general information without specific references.	☐
Reasoning is direct and rational.	☐
Reasoning is indirect, often based on feelings.	☐

Delivery	
Presentations are interactive, lively and entertaining.	☐
Presentations are read and there is no interaction with the audience.	☐
Speakers use notes to present the paper.	☐
Speakers can improvise during a presentation.	☐
The slides contain the text of a presentation.	☐
Presenters use slides to illustrate main points.	☐

Audience response	
Presenters are frequently interrupted with challenging questions.	☐
Questions are asked at the end of presentations.	☐
The audience listen in silence – there are usually very few or no questions.	☐

4 Work in groups. Answer the questions.

1 Have you ever participated in an international conference? Where was it? Did all speakers present in English?
2 Did you notice any cultural differences in presenting material? If yes, what kind?

5 Work in groups. Discuss what behaviour is appropriate in your culture when presenting material at international academic conferences. Use the language of the questionnaire in Activity 3.

Revising what you have learned

6 Think about what you have studied in this unit. Answer the questions. Use the phrases from the Language Support box below.

1 What information was new to you?
2 What have you learned about yourself as a presenter?
3 What skills have you improved?
4 What skills need further improvement?

Language Support: on results and goal-setting

Results	Goal setting
I have managed to …	What I need to improve is …
I think I was good at (+ verb + -*ing*)	I'd like to develop … further.
Now I can (+ verb)	I think my skill of … needs more work.
What I have really improved is …	I plan to develop …
… has become much better.	

Your final presentation

7 Prepare a 10-minute lecture or presentation with visuals to present to your colleagues. Do the tasks below.

1 Think of any topic that is relevant to you. You can continue working on the presentation you planned in this unit, Lesson 2, Activities 10 and 16 on pages 113 and 115.
2 Write a plan of your presentation. Include three main points.
3 Make notes and develop these ideas.
4 Write the text of your presentation or lecture. Pay attention to the structure and phrases that make it easier for the audience to follow you.
5 Check the text for any mistakes.
6 Prepare your slides.
7 Practise the text, and make sure you don't speak for more than 10 minutes. Get ready to present it to the class.
8 Take turns to listen to your colleagues' presentations and ask questions if appropriate.
9 Give your colleagues some feedback using the feedback form on page 130.

Role-play activities

Learner A

Unit 1, Lesson 1, Activity 7

Situation 1 You are a guest at a party at the Consulate/Embassy. Greet the person (Learner B) standing next to you and introduce yourself.

Situation 2 You are sitting in a hotel lobby waiting for a tour bus. A stranger (Learner B) sits down next to you. He/She seems to be waiting for the same bus. He/She starts the conversation by greeting you. Respond to his/her greeting and then introduce yourself.

Situation 3 You have to go down to the welcome dinner organised by the international conference committee. The lift has just stopped on your floor. You walk into the lift and see a stranger (Learner B). Greet him/her, respond to his/her greeting and then introduce yourself.

Situation 4 You have come to a conference and met your old friend at the reception desk. You have not seen each other for two years. Greet him/her and ask about his/her family.

Unit 1, Lesson 2, Activity 7

a Delicious, but too sweet for me.
b Terrible! It was raining 24 hours a day.
c Fantastic! Swimming pool, sauna, everything.
d I love it. Now I have a better salary and excellent prospects.
e Very productive. We have signed a collaboration agreement.
f It was nice to be out of the office for a few days. I learned a lot.

Unit 1, Lesson 2, Activity 8

Situation 1 You are a professor from a British university. You have just arrived. Your Italian colleague is meeting you at the airport.

Situation 2 You watched the film your friend had recommended. You liked it very much. Give your reasons.

Situation 3 You have just returned from an international conference in Thailand, which was a great success. You presented your paper there.

Situation 4 You are a Russian university teacher. You are hosting a foreign guest. You organised an excursion to a Russian monastery for him/her. You want to know if he/she liked the excursion.

Situation 5 You recommended a new mobile application to a tablet/smartphone/iPad to your friend. You want to know if he/she liked the application.

Unit 1, Lesson 4, Activity 11

Situation 1 Invite a visiting professor from Germany out for a coffee after the lecture.

Situation 2 You are an American lecturer visiting a foreign university. Your colleague invites you to a jazz club at the weekend. Thank him/her for the invitation and accept it.

Situation 3 You are at an international conference in Barcelona. The hotel has very good sports facilities. Invite one of the participants from Leeds University to play tennis with you.

Situation 4 You are the head of a group of Indian businessmen visiting a foreign university. Your host invites your group out for a meal tonight. Thank him/her for the invitation and accept it.

Situation 5 You and your friend are from Italy. Learner B is your friend and he/she invites you to his/her country house for the weekend. Thank him/her for the invitation but decline it. Give your reasons.

Situation 6 You are British. Your foreign colleague invites you and your husband/wife to a performance at the local opera house tomorrow evening. Thank him/her for the invitation and accept it.

Situation 7 You want to show your friend from Vietnam round your city. Invite him/her to a walking tour.

Unit 1, Lesson 5, Activity 6

Situation 1 You are in your Estonian colleague's country house. Pay compliments to him/her on his/her house and especially the garden full of flowers.

Situation 2 You are attending an international conference in the University of Economics in Prague. You like the way the conference is organised. Compliment your Czech colleague and thank the organisers.

Situation 3 You have just got your PhD degree. Your friend congratulates you on your achievements. Respond to his/her compliments

Situation 4 You are showing your university facilities to a professor from Denmark. He/She is impressed by a new well-equipped computer centre and a new library. Respond to his/her compliments.

Situation 5 You like the design of the smartphone your friend has just bought. Pay compliments and ask about its options (features and functionality).

Situation 6 Your son/daughter has just entered Cambridge University. You are very proud of him/her and want to share this news with your friend.

Situation 7 You liked your colleague's presentation. Comment on his/her interesting findings and ask about the prospect of further research.

Unit 1, Lesson 6, Activity 7

Situation 1 Your friend is inviting you to go out for a coffee. You can't accept his/her invitation as you are meeting your wife/husband this evening.

Situation 2 The conference organiser reminds you about tonight's dinner for the conference participants. Thank him/her for the invitation and apologise for not coming. You have a train to catch.

Situation 3 You are on the phone to your colleague. You want to discuss the details of your joint presentation. He/She can't talk right now as he/she has an appointment with a doctor. Agree on a time when you can discuss the presentation.

Situation 4 You are having a party for international guests at your house. During the party, one of your guests has to leave. Say goodbye and wish him/her a safe trip back home.

Situation 5 You are having lunch with your foreign colleague. He/She has to leave as he/she has a class. Agree to go out together in the evening.

Unit 2, Lesson 3, Activity 2

When you create slides, you should follow certain requirements. The first slide usually contains [1]_____ . The second slide shows your presentation plan and objectives. The presentation follows a 3.3 rule, which means [2]_____ . It is also important to have a slide with the summary of your presentation and conclusions or results. The last slide contains [3]_____ if anyone would like to contact you afterwards. You should remember that each slide illustrates only one topic.

The titles of the slides should be short, not more than [4]_____ words written in the same style: either all questions or similar phrases. The bulleted lists in the body do not contain full sentences. Usually there are 5–6 words per line. The number of lines on a slide is normally [5]_____ to make it easy for the listeners to follow your ideas. The font *Verdana* size 40 is often used for titles. For the text on slides, suitable fonts are [6]_____ .The text can be accompanied with visuals, but the common rule for slides is 'less is more'.

You can estimate the number of slides if you use the following method: [7]_____ , where *n* is the number of slides and *t* is the time. The beginning should not take longer than 90 seconds. If you want to take questions at the end, you should leave about 25% of your time for them.

Learner B

Unit 1, Lesson 1, Activity 7

Situation 1 You are a guest at a party at the Consulate/Embassy. Respond to the greeting from the person (Learner A) standing next to you. Then introduce yourself.

Situation 2 You are in a hotel lobby waiting to join a tour. You see Learner A sitting in the lobby. He/She seems to be waiting for the same bus. Sit down next to him/her. Start the conversation by greeting the person, respond to his/her greeting and then introduce yourself.

Situation 3 You are in the lift going down to the welcome dinner organised by the international conference committee. The lift stops on the third floor and a stranger (Learner A) walks in and greets you. Respond to his/her greeting and then introduce yourself.

Situation 4 You have come to a conference and met your old friend at the reception desk. You're very glad to see him/her again. You haven't seen each other for two years. Respond to his/her greeting. Answer and ask questions about life.

Unit 1, Lesson 2, Activity 7

g I think it was very interesting. I've made a lot of useful contacts.
h He is nice. Very knowledgeable and helpful.
i Extremely friendly. They asked me a lot of questions.
j Tiring. I had a lot of meetings and phone calls.
k Late as usual. Next time I'll go by train.
l Not bad. But I think I could have presented much better.

Unit 1, Lesson 2, Activity 8

Situation 1 You are an Italian professor. You are meeting your British colleague at the airport.

Situation 2 You recommended a film to your friend. He/She watched it and you want to know what he/she thinks about it.

Situation 3 Your colleague has just returned from an international conference in Thailand where he/she presented his/her paper. You want to know about the conference.

Situation 4 You are a foreign guest at a Russian university. You have just returned from an excursion to a Russian monastery. You liked / didn't like it.

Situation 5 You have just downloaded a new mobile application to your tablet/smartphone/iPad, which your friend recommended to you. You like / don't like it.

Unit 1, Lesson 4, Activity 11

Situation 1 You are a professor from Germany visiting a foreign university. Your colleague invites you for a coffee after the lecture. Thank him/her for the invitation and accept it.

Situation 2 Invite your American colleagues to a jazz club at the weekend.

Situation 3 You are from Leeds University. You attend an international conference in Barcelona. The hotel has very good sports facilities. One of the participants invites you to play tennis with him/her. Thank him/her for the invitation but decline it. Give your reasons.

Situation 4 A group of Indian businessmen are visiting your university. On behalf of the rector invite them out for a meal tonight.

Situation 5 You invite your foreign friends from Italy to your country house for the weekend.

Situation 6 You invite the British professor and his/her wife/husband to a performance at the local opera house tomorrow evening.

Situation 7 You are from Vietnam and you are on a visit to Learners A's country. Your friend invites you to go sightseeing. Thank him/her for the invitation and accept it.

Unit 1, Lesson 5, Activity 6

Situation 1 You have invited your British colleague to your country house. You are showing him/her around the house. You are fond of flowers and you are proud of your garden. Respond to his/her compliments.

Situation 2 You work for the University of Economics in Prague that is hosting an international conference. Your Russian colleague is very pleased with the conference organisation. Respond to his/her compliments.

Situation 3 Your friend has just got a PhD degree. Congratulate him/her on his/her achievements. Mention the quality of the research.

Situation 4 You are a Danish professor visiting a Russian university. Your Russian colleague is showing you around the university. You are impressed by the university facilities, in particular its new, well-equipped computer centre and its new library. Comment on these facilities.

Situation 5 Your have bought a new smartphone and want to know your friend's opinion. Tell him/her about the options (features and functionality) of the phone.

Situation 6 You have heard that your friend's son/daughter has just entered Cambridge University. Congratulate him/her and say something complimentary about his/her son/daughter.

Situation 7 You have presented some preliminary findings of your research. After the presentation your colleague gives some feedback on your presentation. Tell him/her about your plans.

Unit 1, Lesson 6, Activity 7

Situation 1 You would like to talk to your friend about your holiday plans. Suggest going out for a coffee.

Situation 2 You are one of the conference organisers. Remind one of the participants about tonight's dinner and ask if he/she is coming.

Situation 3 Your colleague has called you. She/he wants to discuss the details of your joint presentation. Say sorry and explain that you have to go to the doctor's now. Suggest another time.

Situation 4 You are at a party at your colleague's house. Your taxi has just arrived, and you have to leave the party to go to the airport. Thank Learner A for the party. Say sorry and goodbye.

Situation 5 You are having lunch with your foreign colleague. You have a class in fifteen minutes. Apologise for leaving him/her. Suggest going out in the evening.

Unit 2, Lesson 3, Activity 2

When you create slides, you should follow certain requirements. The first slide usually contains the title of your presentation, your name and the name of the event with date. The second slide shows [1]_____ . The presentation follows a 3.3 rule, which means three parts - an introduction, a body with three main points in it and a conclusion. It is also important to have a slide with [2]_____ .
The last slide contains 'thank-you' and your contact details if anyone would like to contact you afterwards. You should remember that each slide illustrates only [3]_____ .

The titles of the slides should be short, not more than 2–5 words written in the same style: either all questions or similar phrases. The bulleted lists in the body do not contain full sentences. Usually there are [4]_____ words per line. The number of lines on a slide is normally 3 or 4 to make it easy for the listeners to follow your ideas. The font [5]_____ is often used for titles. For the text on slides, suitable fonts are *Arial* or *Tahoma* 28–32. The text can be accompanied with visuals, but the common rule for slides is [6]_____ .

You can estimate the number of slides if you use the following method: $n=t/2$, where n is the number of slides and t is the time. The beginning should not take longer than [7]_____ seconds. If you want to take questions at the end, you should leave about 25% of your time for them.

Slides checklist

Slide heading		Comments
Are the slide titles short and clear?	☐	
Does each slide have the title?	☐	
Slide structure		
Does the outline slide contain only main points?	☐	
Is the order of the outline followed for the rest of the presentation?	☐	
Are the prompts consistent in style?	☐	
Are prompts written in point form?	☐	
Do prompts contain key words?	☐	
Does the conclusion slide:		
• summarise the main points of the presentation?	☐	
• suggest future research? (optional)	☐	
Fonts and colours		
Are fonts large enough for the audience to read?	☐	
Do colours of font and background go well together?	☐	
Spelling and grammar		
Are there any grammatical errors and spelling mistakes?	☐	
Charts, graphs and tables		
Do the graphs have titles?	☐	
Are they easy to read?	☐	
Are they necessary/relevant?	☐	
General comments		
Is the information presented clearly?	☐	
Is there a balance between good design and good content?	☐	

Feedback form

Presenter(s) _____

Title of the presentation _____

Date _____

Criteria	Rating	Comments
Overall impression, purpose achievement	5 4 3 2 1	
Attention-getting opener	5 4 3 2 1	
Outline	5 4 3 2 1	
Structure, organisation, transitions	5 4 3 2 1	
Examples, explanations	5 4 3 2 1	
Visual aids	5 4 3 2 1	
Summary	5 4 3 2 1	
Concluding remarks	5 4 3 2 1	
Eye contact	5 4 3 2 1	
Gestures	5 4 3 2 1	
Volume of voice	5 4 3 2 1	
Pace	5 4 3 2 1	
Enthusiasm	5 4 3 2 1	
Interaction with the audience	5 4 3 2 1	
Q&A	5 4 3 2 1	
Time	5 4 3 2 1	
Other aspects (specify)		

Rating key

1=poor   2=fair   3=acceptable   4=good   5=excellent

Writing

In this module you will:

- write a range of common academic texts
- communicate effectively with colleagues from other countries

Unit 1 Academic correspondence

By the end of this unit you will be able to
➡ follow the rules of formal email etiquette
➡ distinguish between various types of formal letters
➡ organise and structure different types of letter

Lesson 1 Ready to start

Lead-in

1 Work in pairs and discuss these questions.

1 What rules of etiquette do you know?
2 Why is it important to follow these rules?
3 What is email etiquette, in your opinion?

2 Complete the following formal email etiquette rules. Use the words in the list. You can use some verbs more than once. Add *don't* where necessary.

| write | attach | address | be | start | answer | give |

1 _____ the receiver by name or title.
2 _____ a meaningful topic in the subject line.
3 _____ in capitals.
4 _____ your email with a greeting.
5 _____ understandable names to attachments.
6 _____ clear, short paragraphs.
7 _____ friendly and cordial, but _____ familiar.
8 _____ files which are too large.
9 _____ within a reasonable time.

3 Which rules are relevant to your professional life? What rules can you add from your own experience?

Formal style

4 Work in pairs. Mark expressions a–l with *I* if they are part of an informal letter to a friend and *F* if they are from a formal academic letter.

a By the way, are you going to the Statistics Conference, too? If so, I'll take the opportunity to bring you the book you asked for in your previous letter. It's really magnificent. ___
b My name is Professor Copeland, and I am writing to you in order to request information on the Statistics Conference to be held at your University in November, 2015. ___
c Yours faithfully,
   Rebecca Copeland ___
d Dear Jane, ___
e Firstly, could you provide details of the accommodation options? Secondly, I would be grateful if you could provide information on the plenary speakers. ___

f I wonder if you could share the worksheets you designed for teaching Probability, too? It'd be wonderful to use them as well. ___

g Finally, could you please clarify the deadline for registration? ___

h Hope to hear from you soon. ___

i Thank you for in advance for your help with this. I look forward to receiving your reply. ___

j Best wishes,
Rebecca ___

k Hi, there. I hope you're well, and your kids, too. Thanks very much for the teaching materials you sent. I used them with my students and they thought they were great. ___

l Dear Sir or Madam, ___

5 **Put the expressions in order to make two letters. What language features helped you complete the task?**

6 **Tick the features of a formal, academic letter.**

1 Colloquial expressions, that is expressions used in speaking, are numerous (*What's up? Cheers!*). ___

2 Full words, not contractions, are used (*will not* instead of *won't*). ___

3 Words and phrases that connect sentences meaningfully are used. ___

4 The sentences are rather complex. ___

5 Shortened versions of words are used (*u* instead of *you*, *r* instead of *are*). ___

6 Emotional words like *great, superb*, etc. are used. ___

Organising an email / a letter

7 **Put these elements of an email in order.**

a Give relevant information on the subject (What do you want to say?)

b State the aim (Why are you writing?)

c Describe the action you expect from the addressee (What do you want the addressee to do?)

d Close your email/letter politely.

e Open your email/letter with greetings.

8 **Match the expressions 1–8 with their functions a–c.**

a starting an email/letter

b acknowledging receipt of something

c inviting a response

1 I refer to your letter dated …

2 We appreciate your interest in …

3 If you have any further questions, do not hesitate to contact us.

4 Thank you very much for sending the information about …

5 I am writing on behalf of the university to invite you …

6 We look forward to hearing from you soon.

7 I am writing to apply for …

8 Thank you for your letter of …

9 Cover Activity 8 and put the words below in order to make sentences.

1 reply / are / to / your / looking / we / forward
2 our / interest / we / your / appreciate / in / project
3 conference / I / on / writing / am / of / the / the / invite / university / behalf / to / you / to
4 will / early / appreciated / your / confirmation / be
5 contact / do / hesitate / to / us / not

Writing a formal email

10 You have come across an advertisement about a grant for attending a workshop for researchers. Write a short, formal email to the organising committee (100–120 words). Describe your achievements and ask if you fit the criteria to be selected. Use the expressions you have learned in the lesson.

Subject	_____
Opening	_____ ,
Stating the aim	I am writing to you _____ _____
Giving information	_____ _____
Describing the actions you expect	I would be grateful if you could _____ _____
Closing	_____ _____
Signature	_____

Lesson 2 A reference letter

Lead-in

1 Find someone who matches each description below. Report your findings to the class.

a knows what a *reference* is
b has written a reference letter
c has asked their colleagues to write a reference letter for them

Organising a reference letter

2 In Column 1 in the table, tick the features a good reference letter should have.

	1	2
1 Explanation of how long the referee has known the applicant		
2 List of the personal qualities relevant to the specialism		
3 Reference to the applicant's qualifications, experience, and professional skills		
4 The applicant's weaknesses		
5 The applicant's religion, nationality, age, disability and gender		
6 The referee's contact information		

3 Read the letter of reference. In Column 2 in Activity 2, tick the features the letter has.

a Dear Sir/Madam,

b I am Robert Leeds, Professor at Darwin College, University of Nombridge. I am writing in support of Ms Hardworking's application for the MSc in Applied Ecology and Conservation at the University of South Anglia.

I have known this applicant for nearly 15 years, mostly through our shared work on an international ecological project in India.

c Ms Hardworking is a leading professional in India, highly respected for her participation in biodiversity conservation projects. As well as this, she is known as an innovative thinker in the field. She is intelligent, well-read and articulate, and has the maturity, self-discipline and independence to be able to cope with study at postgraduate level. It is typical of her positive attitude and the priority she gives to her professional development that she has chosen to apply for this programme in the middle of a very successful career.

d Moreover, her command of English is native-speaker standard. She has been used to functioning in English since childhood, throughout her education and now in most aspects of her professional life.

e I am pleased to have this opportunity of recommending Ms Hardworking to you as a postgraduate student. She will be an asset to the MSc programme.

f If you have any further questions, feel free to contact me.

Yours faithfully,

Robert Leeds

Professor Robert Leeds

4 Match elements of a reference letter 1–6 with its parts a–f.

1 describing the applicant
2 conclusion
3 summary of what has been written
4 giving more information on the applicant
5 opening
6 describing the referee's position

Language focus

5 Look through the letter of reference again. How do you know it is a positive letter? Find expressions that are used to do the following:

1 describe the professional skills of the applicant
2 describe the applicant's personal qualities and character
3 recommend the applicant to someone else

6 Match positive adjectives 1–4 (with examples) to definitions a–d.

1 mature (*This position would suit a mature specialist with strong computer skills.*)
2 observant (*An observant student noticed the mistake.*)
3 efficient (*She is very efficient: she does everything quickly and well.*)
4 reliable (*You can trust her to take on the most difficult task: she is a reliable person.*)

a able to be trusted or believed
b good or quick at noticing things
c not wasting time or energy
d completely grown or developed

7 In the Language Support box below, you will find more positive words to describe a person. Try to guess the meaning of new words.

Language Support: describing personal qualities

self-confident	competitive
flexible	creative
diplomatic	able to show empathy
imaginative	knowledgeable
energetic	willing to accept responsibility

---

8 Use adjectives from Activity 7 to complete these sentences.

1 Julia is quite _____ because she feels sure about herself and her abilities.
2 Marek is known as a very _____ person because he is good at thinking of new ideas and making new and unusual things.
3 Olga clearly has a desire to become the best and the most successful member of staff, which is quite typical for her _____ personality.
4 Herbert has shown the ability to be _____ and work in different ways, at different times or in different places when it is necessary, to suit new conditions or situations.

Writing a reference letter

9 Imagine one of your students/colleagues asked you to provide a reference for him/her. Think about their main characteristics. Write a reference letter.

10 Work in pairs. Take turns to read each other's letters of reference. Check if all the necessary elements from Activity 4 are included.

Lesson 3 Proposal for partnership

Lead-in

1 Work in pairs and discuss these questions.

1 What partnerships does your department/university have?
2 What is the purpose of a partnership proposal?

Structuring a proposal for partnership

2 In Column 1 in the table, write the numbers to show the order in which you would write these elements in a proposal.

	1	2
a Describing what your institution is working on.		
b Speaking about attachments and contacts.		
c Stating the purpose of your letter.	*1*	
d Writing about the partnerships you already have.		
e Explaining why the partner may be interested in establishing a partnership with you.		

3 Read the proposal for partnership below. What is being proposed? Who do they want to establish a partnership with and why?

Dear Mr Sanchez,

I am writing in hope of establishing a partnership with your institution. I am Alain Lechevre, the executive manager of Lechevre Education. We provide educational programmes in a wide range of subject areas. According to a survey conducted in your region, four colleges have shown interest in developing the research skills of their learners. As we share the same interests, we are honoured to suggest partnering in our Developing Research Skills programme.

The programme is student-friendly and interactive, and students greatly benefit from participating in the project. In addition, we view teaching and research as being not in opposition, but rather as linked with each other.

In the programme, our trainers help students to collect and record information in an organised and professional way, to use data-collection and analysis software competently, to produce well constructed, clear presentations and to use audiovisual aids where appropriate. Furthermore, students are motivated to communicate knowledgeably about their research area and discuss concepts in a scholarly way.

I would like to provide you with a brief outline of the partnerships we have already established. We have already partnered with twenty colleges in the last five years and the results have been very encouraging and fruitful. I am enclosing their feedback. Also, I attach a student's analysis of pre-training and post-training development. This will help you to understand our style of work and see our excellent results.

It would be a pleasure to become associated with an educational institution like yours. You can contact me by phone or by email, should you have any queries about this proposal.

I look forward to hearing from you.

Yours sincerely,
Alain Lechevre

4 In Column 2 of the table in Activity 2, number the elements of the letter as they appear in the proposal.

Language focus

5 In the proposal, find words that collocate with words 1–6 below and match them to definitions a–f.

1 to establish a _____
2 to benefit _____
3 to enclose _____
4 to share _____
5 to have _____ about
6 a brief _____

a to attach information about responses
b to become partners
c to have the advantage of
d a short summary
e to have questions about
f to have common interests

6 Correct the mistakes in the sentences below. Then say in which part of a proposal these sentences can be used. Use the guide in Activity 2 to help you.

1 We have already partnered by a number of educational institutions.
2 I'd like to inform you to our main objectives in the research.
3 I would like to give a brief outline on the advantages of such kind of partnership.
4 I am writing to you because our institution is interested at establishing a partnership to you.
5 I am attaching the feedback at our previous partners.

7 Put the words in order to make sentences for a proposal for partnership. Then put the sentences in order in which they are most likely to appear in a proposal.

1 queries, / by / any / contact / have / me / you / email. / Should
2 to establish / your / willing / a partnership / are / with / We / university.
3 encouraging. / have / The / very / been / results
4 our / I / partners' / enclosing / feedback. / am
5 organisation. / pleasure / would / become / be / your / It / with / a / to / associated
6 provide / already / I / like / you / a brief / of / have / partnerships / we / with / to / the / established. / outline / would

8 Work in pairs. Look at the highlighted words in the proposal in Activity 3, and answer the questions below.

1 What function do these words have?
2 What is the name of this type of word or phrase?

9 What do the highlighted words in Activity 3 have in common?

1 They are used to compare the ideas expressed in two sentences.
2 They are used to contrast the ideas expressed in two sentences.
3 They are used to add information.

10 Complete the paragraph with information that is true for your institution/department.

Our institution provides the opportunity to unite specialists in the field of [1]_____ . [2]_____ give(s) the resources to [3]_____ . Scientists are facilitated to share their expertise and experience in [4]_____ . It enables researchers to implement the innovations in [5]_____ .

11 Redraft the paragraph using the linking words from Activity 3.

Writing a letter of proposal

12 Write a proposal for partnership on behalf of your institution or department. Use the sample letter and examples from the Language focus section.

13 Check your work using the questions below.

1 Have you explained the purpose of your letter?
2 Have you described your institution/department?
3 Have you outlined the benefits of potential partnership?
4 Have you provided information for further contacts?
5 Have you thanked your potential partner?
6 Is the letter written in a formal style?

Lesson 4 Writing a covering letter for a grant proposal

Lead-in

1 Imagine that you have found someone who might be able to fund your research project. What will you write in a covering letter to make a good first impression? Work in pairs to make a list.

2 Complete the sentences with words from the list. One word is used twice.

> goals   proposal   institution (x2)   research

Information to be included in a covering letter:

1 A description of your _____ .
2 A statement explaining how you will help accomplish the funder's _____ .
3 An explanation of the rationale and purpose of your _____ .
4 An explanation of why the grant-awarding foundation is a fit with your _____ .
5 A 'thank you' for the opportunity to submit the _____ .

Structuring a covering letter

3 Read the email and answer the questions.

1 What do we learn about the applicant's organisation?
2 What is funding requested for?
3 How do they plan to achieve their aim?

Dear Mr Peeler,

On behalf of the Department of History, Cultural Studies and Ethnology, I am pleased to present this grant proposal for our project, titled 'Archives of Vologda monasteries and churches of the XV–XVII centuries'. It aims to complete our research work on compiling a list of documents from church archives in the Vologda region.

We are requesting financial assistance to enable us to organise trips to Saint Petersburg (to the Russian National Library) and Kiev (to the Ukrainian National Library) where we can get access to rare books and manuscripts about the history of our region for the period mentioned above.

We appreciate this opportunity to apply, as we consider this grant an important factor in the development of the whole nation. Please contact me if you have any questions about our work or our proposal.

Sincerely,
Dr Marina Okasova, Assistant Professor

---

4 Look again at the sentences in Activity 2 and check if all the information is included in the letter above.

Language focus

5 Underline phrases in the letter which match these functions.

1 giving contact information
2 introducing the reasons for funding
3 thanking the funder
4 introducing your organisation
5 describing the purpose of your project

6 Match the pairs of expressions A–E to functions 1–5 from Activity 5.

A _____

- In our department, we deal with ...
- Among our main activities are ....

B _____

- The long-term/short-term plan is/was designed to ...
- The purpose/goal of the proposed project is to ...

C _____

- Our organisation receives funding from state, city and federal sources. We need assistance/support in ...
- Your assistance will enable us to...

D _____

- Thank you for the guidance and help in the development of our project.
- We are grateful for the opportunity to apply for the grant.

E _____

- Should you have any questions or require further/additional information, please contact ...
- For answers to any questions about our project/application, please feel free to...

7 Complete the sentences with words from Activity 6.

1 If you are asking money for a short period of time, you want to receive _____ financing.
2 If you need financial help, you require the funder's financial _____.
3 The funder will contact you if they require _____ information (i.e. more information on the project).
4 When you are _____ to someone, you thank them for what they have done.

Writing a covering letter

8 Read the Table of Contents of a grant proposal (see Reading module Unit 4, page 55). Write a covering letter for the proposal.

9 Go to Activity 2 to check if all the elements are included in your covering letter.

Unit 2 Writing a summary

By the end of this unit you will be able to

⇒ organise a summary

⇒ evaluate a summary

⇒ write a summary of an academic article

Lesson 1 What makes a good summary?

Lead-in

1 Work in pairs and discuss the questions.

1 Have you ever written a summary?
2 Why do we write them?
3 How long should a summary be?

Organising a summary

2 In Column 1, tick the features you think a summary should have.

	1	2
1 The author's name and the title of the article		
2 Graphs and tables		
3 Detailed explanations		
4 The author's main idea		
5 Details to support the idea		
6 Your own views on the problem		
7 As much of the original text as possible		
8 Quotations		
9 Formal expressions, linking words		

3 Read the example summary below and say what kind of misunderstanding takes place in a college classroom.

In his article 'No Allusions in the Classroom,' Jaime O'Neill emphasises the existing misunderstanding between students and teachers in a college classroom. He claims that teachers assume their students have basic knowledge they do not really possess. Moreover, students do not ask questions because they do not want to show their ignorance. O'Neill supports his conclusions by the results of the general knowledge test he administered to his students, which they answered more incorrectly than correctly. The author adds that, according to recent polls, a large portion of adults in the US are ignorant about the history of the country and the planet they live on. Finally, O'Neill expresses his opinion that instructors should be responsible for giving general information to their students.

4 In Column 2 in Activity 2, tick the features which are included in this summary.

Language focus

5 The words in the list are often used to report what other people say or think. Add at least three more verbs from the summary above.

state   inform   argue   mention   point out
suggest   demonstrate   discuss   believe

6 Say which sentences in the summary in Activity 3 are used to:

1 introduce the main ideas of the original
2 provide an author's point of view
3 finish the summary

7 In expressions a–h underline the reporting verbs. Circle the words and phrases that show the order of events.

a At the beginning of the article the author points out/emphasises ...
b Next / Further on, the following problems/issues are raised ...
c In addition, the reader is informed about ...
d Then, the following points are examined/studied: ...
e The author suggests/assumes/claims that ...
f Summing up the author's thoughts ...
g Finally, the author concludes/assumes that ...
h The research the author conducted demonstrated that ...

8 Match phrases a–h in Activity 7 to functions 1–3 in Activity 6. Sometimes there may be more than one possible answer.

9 Read the summary below. Is the original article positive or negative about the educational reforms?

John Tierney, in 'The Coming Revolution in Public Education', **1** e_____ the belief that the educational reforms in the USA are harmful. The author **2** i_____ us that, as a result of the reform initiatives, standardised tests and assessments have been introduced in public schools and teachers held accountable for the results. The reforms, he **3** a_____ , also recommend controlling classroom instruction. He then points out that the reforms have profit motives and involve corporate interests. Further on the reader is informed about the negative reaction of the public and teachers to these reforms. The author **4** s_____ that teachers should be given more autonomy and respected as professionals. Tierney then **5** a_____ that standardisation leads to the loss of individuality and diversity. Finally, the author **6** a_____ that public education is not aimed at bringing in money, and that is why business should not be involved. As a conclusion, Tierney **7** s_____ that these kinds of reforms should be opposed.

10 Complete the summary with reporting verbs from Activities 3, 5 and 7. The first letter of each verb is given.

11 Read the notes about the main ideas of an article. Write a summary using reporting verbs and linking words.

- author: James Vernon
- title: 'Open online courses – an avalanche that might just get stopped'
- online education through massive open online courses (MOOCs) is not always as good as it may seem
- if offered free, MOOCs bring in no money and can even fail to cover their costs
- the quality of education cannot be effectively monitored and controlled
- if businesses sell the MOOCs, low-achieving students have access to higher education
- academics are not enthusiastic about online higher education

---

Lesson 2 Topic sentences

Lead-in

1 What is a topic sentence? Where do you find it in a paragraph?

Writing a summary

2 Read the article by Tonya Troka and say why more people nowadays prefer to study online.

The future of online education

Distance education has been around from the 1800s. Correspondence courses helped people learn trades in their own free time, while radio and taped television courses later educated students in remote areas. Now, with the rapid expansion and evolution of the internet, online education has become commonplace. It's now possible to earn a degree from an accredited college without ever setting foot on campus, and more people enroll every year. According to the Sloan Consortium's report 'Changing Course: Ten Years of Tracking Online Education in the United States,' more than 6.7 million students were taking at least one online course during the fall 2011 term, an increase of 570,000 students over the previous year.

Higher education, in general, has grown significantly. In 1975, 21.9 % of Americans had a Bachelor's degree. In 2011, 38.7 % of Americans between the ages of 25 and 64 had earned a two- or four-year college degree. The main driver behind the increase in higher education is the huge change in the overall economy of the U.S. over the last fifty years. Most workers are now employed by the service sector, where more specialized skills are often a necessary requirement for finding a job. As a result, some post-secondary education is now seen as critical for workplace viability by a majority of the population.

And the majority of the population is now online. In 1997, less than 20% of U.S. households had internet access. By 2011, that percentage had grown to 71.7 %. As with music, television, and newspapers, higher education needs to move to where the people are if it wants to expand its user base. Also, traditional campuses are having trouble maintaining facilities that meet the growing college population's needs. While the cost savings of running an online degree program aren't tremendous, it's generally easier for colleges to move programs online than it is for them to build extensions to their campuses.

The Sloan Consortium's findings reveal that many institutions expect more working adults to turn to continuing education online to build new skills or enhance existing ones to better their chances in the job marketplace, and also to avoid paying higher fuel costs as commuter students. Every year has seen an increase in the proportion of total enrollments that are online, starting at 11.7% in 2003 and increasing to 32% in 2011. The convenience of being able to complete a degree at a reduced impact to personal and professional life makes online education attractive to working adults. As adults strive to continue earning, they'll want to continue learning. And they'll continue gravitating to ways that fit their lifestyle.

3 Underline the topic sentence in each paragraph. Compare your ideas in pairs.

4 Look through the text again and underline ideas, supporting details and facts you could include in a summary of this text.

5 Work in pairs. Read the two summaries below. Which summary reflects the text better?

1

In her 'The Future of Online Education' Tonya Troka provides the reasons for the growing popularity of learning via the internet. The author mentions the results of surveys that demonstrate that the number of people taking part in on-line courses is growing. She stresses that nowadays there is an increased demand for educated specialists, and on-line education gives an opportunity to receive a diploma without leaving work. Moreover, the author suggests that this type of education is convenient for Universities, as its cost is rather low. Finally, the author states that on-line education is a good alternative for working adults.

2

The text under consideration is written by Tonya Troka. The purpose of the article is to give readers information about the growing amount of online education. Based on convincing data the author proves the idea that online courses are a convenient and attractive way to get a degree or to continue education without giving up employment. The author also stresses the fact that traditional campuses are having trouble maintaining facilities that meet the growing college population's needs. Troka finishes her article by stating that as adults strive to continue earning, they'll want to continue learning.

6 Compare Summaries 1 and 2. Tick the correct boxes in the first and second columns.

	Summary 1	Summary 2	Summary 3
1 The summary is short.			
2 The summary reflects the main idea of the author.			
3 The title of the article and the author's name are included.			
4 Some examples to support the main idea are included.			
5 It is written in language different from the author's.			
6 There are no detailed explanations.			
7 Quotations are not included.			
8 The summary is written in a formal style.			

7 Suggest improvements for the less successful summary.

8 Write a summary for an article from the Reading Module, Unit 2.

9 Work in pairs. Read your partner's summary critically. Tick the column for Summary 3 in the checklist in Activity 6. Give feedback to your partner.

Unit 3 Writing an abstract

By the end of this unit you will be able to

➡ structure an abstract

➡ connect parts of an abstract using linking words

➡ notice particular features of abstracts from different fields of study

➡ write an abstract for an article

Lesson 1 Make your abstract cohesive

Lead-in

1 How often do you write articles? What else do you have to write when you submit an article?

2 Work in groups and complete the spidergram about your experience of writing abstracts.

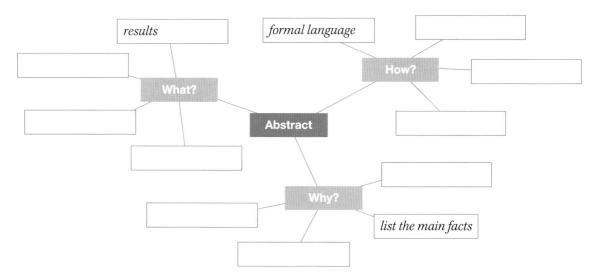

Structure of an abstract

3 Match the parts of an abstract (1–5) to the questions they answer (a–e).

1 background   **a** What was the purpose of the research?
2 aims   **b** What were the main findings?
3 approach   **c** What did the research lead to?
4 results   **d** What was the context of the work?
5 conclusion   **e** What were the methods used in the research?

4 Match sentences a–e to abstract parts 1–5 in Activity 3.

a The findings of the research illustrate how / show the impact of ...; We can predict/ foresee that ...

b We conducted the studies of / experiments on...; We employed the following methods ...; The research explored ...; We tested this hypothesis using ...

c This article is motivated by ...; ... is a fundamental question in ...; Previous research indicates / has shown that / has focused on ...

d This article has the following goals/objectives ...; The article examines/studies ...; The main purpose of the article is to ...

e The findings support the prediction/model ...; Theoretical contributions and practical implications are discussed/presented ...

5 Read this article abstract and say if the authors agree that having more computers at school leads to changes in teaching.

> Your notes
>
> Most policy makers, corporate executives, practitioners, and parents assume that wiring schools, buying hardware and software, and distributing the equipment throughout will lead to abundant classroom use by teachers and students and improved teaching and learning. This article examines these assumptions in two high schools located in the heart of technological progress, Northern California's Silicon Valley. Our qualitative methodology included, firstly, interviews with teachers, students, and administrators, secondly, classroom observations, review of school documents, and, finally, surveys of both teachers and students in the two high schools. We found that although teachers used computers for classroom work, access to equipment and software seldom led to widespread teacher and student use and most teachers were occasional users or non-users. As a result, more often their use sustained rather than altered existing patterns of teaching practice. We offer two interrelated explanations for these challenges to the dominant assumptions that guide present technological policy making. In general, traditions in high schools will influence the slow revolution in teaching practices.

6 Divide the abstract into the five parts listed in Activity 3. Write the names of the parts in the left-hand column.

Language focus

7 Find the following words in the abstract.

1 the word that is close in meaning to these verbs: *to believe, to imagine, to suppose*
2 the word that is opposite in meaning to these verbs: *to collect, to gather*
3 the verb that is close in meaning to these verbs: *to investigate, to study*
4 a noun that comes from the verb *to assume*
5 a pair of verbs, one of which means *continued*, and the other means *changed*

8 Underline the phrases which helped you identify the parts of the abstract. Explain your answers, e.g.:

The phrase 'Most policy makers' shows that the author has read a number of papers and now presents this information as a background of the research.

9 Work in pairs. Decide what functions the highlighted words in the abstract have.

10 Read the examples of linking words in the Language Support box. Say what the underlined words mean. Fill in the gaps with the highlighted words from the abstract.

Language Support: linking words

- Words used to <u>enumerate</u>: *initially,* _____ , _____ , *third(ly), next,*
_____ .

- Words that express <u>causation</u>: *thus,* _____ , *because, therefore.*
- Words that express <u>contrasts</u> and <u>comparisons</u>: _____ , *however, whereas,*
likewise, in contrast.
- Words used to <u>generalise</u>: *overall,* _____ , *in short, to conclude, generally*

---

11 Put the letters in order to make a word with the same function as the linking words in the right-hand column.

1	_____ (utsh)	in this way, hence, so
2	_____ (eeeortfrh)	as a result, for that reason, consequently
3	_____ (iiwsklee)	also, similarly, additionally
4	_____ (ehewrov)	but, still, nevertheless, nonetheless, although
5	_____ (frthomueerr)	in addition, moreover, besides
6	_____ (iiiytnall)	at first, at the beginning
7	_____ (llrvaoe)	on the whole, generally

12 Read the abstract below and say how the use of technology in university classes influences the way students study.

The trend toward technology enhanced classrooms has escalated quickly during the past five years as students have become increasingly tech savvy. **1**_____ classrooms across the nation have become 'wired' and textbook publishers now offer a wide variety of computerised teaching supplements. In fact, some may argue that the use of technology is now expected in the college classroom. The objective of this research is to examine whether the use of technology in university classes impacts student behaviour and student perceptions of instructional quality. This paper summarises the results of a survey administered to students enrolled in business courses at a mid-sized Midwestern university. The results suggest that adding technology in courses where it is not currently used is likely to have a positive impact on student perceptions of the instructor and on student behavior. **2**_____ , removing technology from courses that already use it would not appear to have a negative impact on all aspects of student behaviour. **3**_____ there are certain aspects of student behaviour which appear to be technology neutral: firstly, the amount of time that students study, **4**_____ the quantity of notes they take, **5**_____ their attendance, and, **6**_____ , their interaction with the instructor. **7**_____ , technology tends to have a meaningful impact on student preparation for class, attentiveness, quality of notes taken, student participation in class, student learning, desire to take additional classes from the instructor or in the subject matter, and **8**_____ the overall evaluation of the course and the instructor.

---

13 Fill in the gaps in the abstract in Activity 12 with a suitable linking word/phrase from the list. There is one extra word which you do not need to use.

also	however	as a result	secondly	initially
thirdly	in contrast	finally	overall	

14 Match the highlighted words in the abstract to their synonyms 1–10 below.

1 assumed

2 influences

3 communication

4 improved, made better

5 will probably have

6 became higher

7 aim

8 given to

9 parts

10 study

15 Complete the sentences below with the highlighted words/phrases from the abstract.

1 The main purpose of the article is to describe the ___enhanced___ procedure of the research.

2 This article is motivated by a series of experiments on the _____ between peers in a group.

3 Previous research indicates that the tension between the two countries has _____ .

4 The article aims to _____ some aspects of the problem described.

5 We conclude that a wider use of the gadget can be _____ .

6 We can foresee that the study _____ to have similar results in other settings.

7 The poll has been _____ a group of University teachers.

8 The _____ of the study is to examine the reasons for such behaviour.

9 It is demonstrated how global warming _____ the environment.

10 The paper presents moral _____ of the biotechnological experiments.

Describing research

16 Think about the research you are carrying out or have already completed. Finish the sentences below to describe it.

- We conducted a study of _____ .
- Numerous research in the area show _____ .
- Our objective was to examine _____ .
- Firstly, _____ used.
- Secondly, _____ was examined.
- In addition, _____ was/were demonstrated.
- Overall, _____ .
- Finally, the following conclusion was drawn: _____ .

Lesson 2 Abstracts from different fields of study

Lead-in

1 There are eight words connected with abstracts hidden below. Work in pairs to find them. Say what each word means.

S	R	E	S	U	L	T	S	A	C	H	X
X	C	O	A	B	S	T	R	A	C	T	O
M	B	V	P	A	D	B	I	I	J	N	Q
N	A	T	P	Z	P	R	P	M	H	Z	M
R	F	O	R	M	A	L	K	S	N	G	S
H	K	J	O	I	M	O	L	M	T	R	I
G	G	B	A	C	K	G	R	O	U	N	D
C	O	N	C	L	U	S	I	O	N	H	R
C	O	Z	H	B	S	T	R	A	C	T	E
K	U	L	I	N	K	E	R	S	S	C	E

Spot the difference

2 Match abstracts A–C to fields of study 1–3.

1 Pure Science
2 Social Sciences
3 Humanities

A

> In this article I consider whether Hegel is a naturalist or an anti-naturalist with respect to his philosophy of nature. I adopt a cluster-based approach to naturalism, on which positions are more or less naturalistic depending how many strands of the cluster *naturalism* they exemplify. I focus on two strands: belief that philosophy is continuous with the empirical sciences, and disbelief in supernatural entities. I argue that Hegel regards philosophy of nature as distinct, but not wholly discontinuous, from empirical science and that he believes in the reality of formal and final causes insofar as he is a realist about universal forms that interconnect to comprise a self-organising whole. Nonetheless, for Hegel, natural particulars never fully realise these universal forms, so that empirical inquiry into these particulars and their efficient–causal interactions is always necessary. In these two respects, I conclude, Hegel's position sits in the middle of the naturalism/anti-naturalism spectrum.

B

> This research assessed phonological and morphological awareness in dyslexic university students. We tested 44 dyslexic university students in phonological and morphological awareness tasks and compared their performances. In the phonological awareness tests, the dyslexic university students performed at the same level as their reading level controls. In contrast, they systematically outperformed their reading level controls in the morphological awareness tasks and almost reached the proficiency level of the chronological age controls. The results show that dyslexic university students develop their morphological awareness more than their phonological awareness. These findings add to the evidence indicating that morphological awareness is not deficient in dyslexia and could instead play a beneficial role in the development of literacy skills in this population.

C

> A process capable of producing large amounts of energy by a nuclear fusion process between nickel and hydrogen, occurring below 1,000 K, is described. Experimental values of the ratios between output and input energies obtained in a certain number of experiments are reported. The occurrence of the effect is justified on the basis of existing experimental and theoretical results. Measurements performed during the experiments allow for the exclusion of neutron and gamma ray emissions.

3 Read the abstracts again and match them to statements 1–8.

The abstract ...

1 includes the following parts: Aims, Results.
2 includes the following parts: Aims, Approach, Conclusion.
3 includes the following parts: Aims, Approach, Results, Conclusion.
4 discusses the approach of a well-known theorist.
5 is written in the passive voice.
6 is written in the first person singular.
7 presents opinions.
8 describes objective results.

Language focus

4 In the abstracts, find words/phrases similar in meaning to definitions 1–7. The letters show you in which abstract the word is used.

1 think about, reflect, give attention (A) _____
2 in connection with something (A) _____
3 accept, use (A) _____
4 component, aspect, feature (A) _____
5 judge the importance or value of something (B) _____
6 reasons for believing that something is or is not true (B) _____
7 show that something is right or reasonable (C) _____

5 Use the words from Activity 4 to complete the gaps in sentences 1–7.

1 There is no scientific _____ that a person's character is reflected in their handwriting.
2 It's too early to _____ the long-term consequences of the experiment.
3 We _____ two factors which determine the most appropriate way of planning the project.
4 We _____ a well-known model of the economy development.
5 The attempt is made to _____ the existence of this science to professional and academic communities.
6 There are a number of _____s in feminist thinking.
7 I am writing _____ your letter of 15 June.

6 In abstracts A–C, find words/phrases that are used to do the following.

1 to describe the research (e.g. *I focus on, this paper presents*)
2 to write about actions (e.g. *tested, a comparison is carried out*)
3 to describe the results (e.g. *the results show*)

7 Underline the passive constructions in the abstracts. Why is the passive voice used?

8 In Abstract C, in the sentences in the passive voice, find the parts of the sentences which name the object of the research. Are they individual words or phrases?

9 Underline the phrases in these sentences which describe the object of the research. Then rewrite the sentences in the passive voice.

a We examine the impact of social networks on society.
b We consider the ways of interaction in the modern academic environment.
c We focus on the process capable of producing large amounts of energy.
d We justify the use of the approach described.
e We perform the measurements of output and input energies.

10 Edit the following abstract.

1 Complete gaps 1–5 with the correct words from Activity 4.
2 Rewrite underlined sentences a–d using the passive voice.
3 Add linking words where appropriate.

The expansion of higher education systems, new demands on institutions and growing pressures on resources have become common trends across most developed countries. (**a**) This paper explores the early career paths of academics. (**b**) It makes initial comparisons between different higher education systems. (**c**) We have written this paper with ¹_____ to the *Changing Academic Profession* study. This study ²_____ s the following facts: respondents' degrees, age at which they qualified, disciplines they studied and now teach. The conditions of academic work are ³_____ ed. The collected data ⁴_____ various degrees of flexibility and mobility required of academics in the early and later stages of their careers. The study provides ⁵_____ that academics are becoming more mobile domestically and internationally. Academics from the 17 countries in the study are quite satisfied with the technical resources provided by their institutions. (**d**) They criticise the personnel and funds available to support teaching and research.

---

11 In abstracts A–C, find sentences written in the first person. Why is the first person used in these cases? Finish the sentences below to express your own opinions and describe your research.

1 I/We consider _____ to be _____
2 I/We adopt a _____ approach to _____
3 In my paper I/we focus on _____
4 I/We argue that _____
5 I/We conclude that _____

Writing an abstract

12 Put these steps for writing an abstract in order.

a __1__ Read through the paper and choose sentences with key ideas.
b _____ Give the abstract to a colleague and ask him/her whether it makes sense
c _____ Check that your abstract conveys only the essential information.
d _____ Read your rough draft and delete extra words and phrases (examples, jargon, opinions and detailed descriptions).
e _____ Organise the information you have gathered into an initial rough draft.
f _____ Check to see if it meets the guidelines of the targeted journal. Count the words.
g _____ Read the abstract as if you were another researcher deciding whether to read your paper.
h _____ Write the final version of the abstract.

13 Write an abstract for one of the following.

1 an article you have written (the article may be written in your native language)
2 an article you studied in the Reading module, Unit 3

14 Work in pairs. Read your partner's abstract. Think about the questions below. Then give feedback.

1 Why did he/she do this study or project?
2 What did he/she do and how?
3 What did he/she find?
4 What do his/her findings mean?
5 If he/she suggested a new method, how well did it work?
6 Did he/she use formal vocabulary?
7 Did he/she use linking words to connect ideas?

15 Rewrite your abstract, using your partner's suggestions.

Unit 4 Writing an executive summary of a grant proposal

By the end of this unit you will be able to

⇒ recognise characteristics of a grant proposal

⇒ structure an executive summary of a grant proposal

⇒ recognise features of formal and informal writing

⇒ analyse and use appropriate language for writing an executive summary of a grant proposal

⇒ write essential parts of an executive summary of a grant proposal

Lesson 1 A grant proposal

Lead-in

1 Work in pairs and answer the questions below.

1 Have you ever applied for a grant? If yes, was it an international or an internal grant? If it was an international grant, did you need any help to fill in the application forms?
2 Have you ever had to write a grant application or proposal in English?
3 What do you think helps to get funding for an academic project?

2 Read what funders sometimes say when refusing grant proposals (1–3) and choose one recommendation from statements a–f to avoid each reason for refusal.

1
> Sorry, but we don't think the problem raised in your proposal is serious.

2
> We doubt whether it is possible to implement your project within the proposed period of time.

3
> Sorry, but our fund is trying to achieve slightly different goals.

a You should provide a clear proposal with an exact time-frame and the expected results of the research.
b You should present clear objectives of your research project.
c Your research purposes should correspond with the aims of a grant funder.
d You should propose a solution to an important and critical problem.
e You should find additional funding to your project.
f Your proposal should contain detailed information about how you intend to conduct it.

Executive summary

3 Read the characteristics of an executive summary and tick the ones that make it attractive to funders. Compare your answers with a partner.

1 It provides a description of the project and expected results.
2 It gives the correct contact information.
3 It is very detailed and backed up by statistics.
4 It concentrates on the main point of your project, not all the side issues.
5 It may include a time chart and project organisation chart if there is space.
6 It clearly states what is expected from the funder.
7 It includes the one, best, most creative aspect (the 'hook') of the project.
8 It clearly states what your organisation and other partners are investing in the project.

4 Read this executive summary and say what they want funding for.

Step to Success

Marie Crump, Special Educational Needs Coordinator

^a <u>Mission statement</u>

The mission of the 'Step to Success' project is to improve students' academic performance in Lightwood High School. We are seeking a grant to help students with special educational needs to stimulate their autonomous learning. The objective is that by the end of the year they will have developed their cognitive skills up to the level of their peers. The project is based on the latest research on how to create an effective inclusive educational environment.

b _____

Lightwood High School faces problems caused by the growing number of students having learning difficulties. Our study shows that 78 students out of 342 suffer from attention deficit disorder and mental deficiency, leading to low academic achievement. [1]*Also / Additionally*, if these students [2]*are not given / aren't given* an opportunity to improve their cognitive skills, they are more likely to miss classes or commit offences.

c _____

Our school will provide students with access to computers equipped with special educational software. Students will be able to implement various tasks presented in computer games. Standardised tests will be conducted at the beginning of the project to [3]*identify / find out* the students' cognitive level. Finally, at the end of the school year, they will be assessed to determine their level of improvement.

d _____

The 'Step to Success' project hopes to enable students with special needs [4]*to make better / to enhance* their cognitive skills in order to prepare them for further education. The project aims to help these students access the general curriculum and attend regular classes with their peers, so they can [5]*go on / continue* learning in an inclusive environment.

e _____

Funding of €10,300 is requested [6]*to implement this programme / to put this programme into action* and for the purchase of special educational software and hardware for the school's classroom. The budget includes funds for ten computers and programmes. This will enable ten independent desks, which will give students flexibility in working hours

5 Match headings 1–4 to sections b–e of the executive summary.

1 Budget
2 Problem statement / Statement of need
3 Expected results
4 Project summary / Project description

Formal style

6 Read this text and compare it with part (a) of the text in Activity 4. Which one is more formal? How do you know?

> Our idea is to improve students' academic performance in Lightwood High School. We're looking for a grant to help weak students to do well and stimulate their autonomous learning. So, how do we formulate our objective? By the end of the year we want them to have developed their cognitive skills up to the level of their fellows. Luckily, the project is based on the latest research on how to create good inclusive educational environment.

7 Read the general guidelines for writing in a formal style. Use them to explain why certain words/phrases in the text in Activity 6 are inappropriate.

1 Avoid adverbs that show personal attitude (e.g. *unfortunately, surprisingly*).
2 Avoid too informal vocabulary (idiomatic or colloquial expressions, e.g. *thank goodness, kids*).
3 Avoid an informal use of multi-word verbs (phrasal verbs) when there is a suitable synonym (e.g. *set up = install*).
4 Avoid contracted forms (e.g. *can't, won't*).
5 Avoid rhetorical questions (e.g. *And why does it happen?*).

8 In the text in Activity 4, choose the more formal options (1–6).

A mission statement

9 Put the words in order to make sentences about the mission of an organisation.

1 is / high quality care and services / Our mission / to our members / to provide
2 in the city / to reduce / is / air pollution / Our goal
3 the development / Our primary focus / distance-learning courses / on / of / online / is
4 safely / electricity / The purpose / to deliver / is
5 is to serve / higher learning / Our aim / society / as a centre of
6 an increase of access to / programmes / Our institution / higher education / is responsible for

10 Which sentences from Activity 9 use the to-infinitive to state the mission? Which ones use a noun phrase?

11 Think about a grant proposal you or your institution could make. Complete the model below in a formal style.

The mission of _____ is to _____ .

Our objective is to _____ .

We are responsible for _____ .

Our primary focus in on _____ .

We will _____ .

Stating a problem

12 Read a problem statement from an executive summary for a grant proposal. Answer the questions.

1 What is the main problem?
2 Who is affected by this problem?
3 How was the problem discovered?
4 What can help to solve the problem?

There is a tremendous need, especially for high-risk youth in low-income neighbourhoods, for programs that ¹_____ (provide) activities and support for children during the after school hours. In 1998, the Children's Defence Fund ²_____ (report) that violent crime by young people aged 10–17 peaks between 3 and 7 p.m. Previous research has shown that children and teens in poor neighbourhoods are struggling for direction and positive opportunities ³_____ (need) to keep them safe. In addition, a study published in *Pediatrics* magazine ⁴_____ (find) that eighth graders who ⁵_____ (leave) alone after school reported greater use of cigarettes, marijuana, and alcohol than those in adult-supervised settings.

Current research ⁶_____ (indicate) that supervised after-school programs keep children safe and out of trouble. By implementing our project, we intend to enhance their academic achievement significantly.

13 Complete the sentences with the correct form of the verbs in brackets: active or passive.

14 Underline the phrases in the text which have a similar meaning to the phrases below.

1 Studies indicated that ...
2 A survey/An experiment showed that ...
3 We plan to improve ...
4 Present research states that ...
5 Prior research has reported that ...
6 There is a huge demand for projects which ...

15 Write the problem statement for your grant proposal. Answer the questions below.

1 Why is your project worth doing?
2 How did you decide that the problem exists?
3 Who/What does the problem affect?
4 What have other researchers done in this field?
5 What will your new work add to the field of knowledge? How is it innovative?

Lesson 2 Polishing an executive summary

Lead-in

1 Work in pairs. Complete the sentences.

1 If you want to get funding for your research project, you should ...
2 If you want to write a successful grant proposal, you should ...
3 Your execurive summary of a grant proposal should consist of ...
4 The style you write your proposal in is ...
5 When writing a grant proposal, you should avoid ...
6 In order to present your organisation, you should ...
7 When stating a problem, it is recommended to ...

Project summary

2 Read the following project summary and choose the best title for the proposed project.

A Development of relationships between America and Madagascar.
B Evolution of the reproductive system in primates.
C Major differences between lemurs and lorises.

[a]We will analyse the anatomical, behavioural, and physiological differences among lemurs and lorises and the social and ecological [1]*things / traits* that influence these differences. [b]The proposed research will [2]*address / look into* three topics of great significance to understanding primate biology and evolution: (1) comparative anatomy of the reproductive system, (2) evolutionary changes in the reproductive system, and (3) rates of evolution. [c]The anatomical, behavioural, and ecological characters generated [3]*here / in this study* will be used to test functional and evolutionary hypotheses about the reproductive system that [4]*could not / couldn't* be tested with existing data.

[d]The proposed research involves international, collaborative research between scientists from the US and Madagascar. [e]The results of this study will be of [5]*major / big* importance both for the conservation of endangered species in the wild as well as the maintenance of captive colonies involved in biomedical research. [f]The results of this study will be incorporated [6]*at once / immediately* into educational programmes in both countries. [g]Because this research involves attractive and endangered species, the results of this work are likely to be of considerable public interest and will reach a broad public audience.

lemurs and lorises = small animals similar to monkeys (primates) with thick fur and a long tail, which live in trees and are active at night
reproductive = relating to the process of having babies or producing plants
incorporate = to include something as part of something larger
endangered = animals or plants that may soon not exist because there are very few left alive

3 In the text in Activity 2, choose the more formal words or phrases in options1–6. Compare your answers with a partner.

4 Read the text again and match sentences a–g with the questions below.

1 Who will carry out the project? ___
2 What is the significance of the project? ___
3 How will the results of the research be applied? ___
4 What is the specific objective of the project? ___
5 What methods will be used to prove research hypotheses? ___
6 What is the main purpose of the research? ___
7 Who might be interested in the research results? ___

5 Paraphrase the project summary in Activity 2, using phrases from the Language Support box.

Language Support: project summaries

... will provide ...
The project starts with ... The next step is ... Finally, ...
Extra effort will be made to ...
Special attention will be paid to ...
The plan will include ...
This project will be completed within/in/over ... (period of time)

---

6 Write the project summary for a grant proposal. Use the Language Support box to help you.

7 Work in pairs. Read your partner's project summary. Does it contain the following information?

- a brief background of the project
- specific aims, objectives or hypotheses
- significance of the proposed research
- unique features and innovation of the project
- methods (action steps) to be used
- a description of how results will influence other research areas

Expected results

8 Read the text in Activity 2 again and find sentences about the results of the project. Answer the questions below.

1 What tenses are used in these sentences?
2 Which tense expresses a promise?
3 Which structure indicates that the author is not sure about the results?
4 Which structure would you choose to present your expected results?

9 Read the text below and say what the outcomes of the proposed research are. Then fill in the gaps with a suitable verb.

> will offer   will have   will promote   will provide

The research ¹_____ interdisciplinary understanding of urban green spaces from the ecological and sociological viewpoints. In addition, the outcomes of the research ²_____ important and applicable knowledge and tools for the planners and decision makers of urban land use planning. Furthermore, the research process ³_____ collaboration between researchers, land-use officials, residents and other stakeholders. Although the research takes place in Finland, it ⁴_____ international relevance, especially as the project has extensive international collaboration.

10 Study the Language Support box and find words to complete the crossword.

Language Support: expected results

We expect to achieve ...
The main expectation of the project / research is ...
The results of the research will be published in academic journals (e.g. ...).
The results of the project might be recommended to (scientists, students) in the field of (subject).
... will benefit from ...

Down
1 to make research findings available to people, especially in a book or magazine (verb)
2 to suggest using research findings for further studies (verb)
3 to be in a better position because you can use the research results (verb)
4 a serious magazine that is published regularly about a particular subject (noun)
5 an area of activity or interest (noun)

Across
6 to succeed in finishing something or reaching an aim (verb)
7 product, outcome, effect of the research (noun)
8 assumption, belief, prediction (noun)

11 Think about your research project and present its expected results in writing. Use the Language Support box in Activity 10 to help you.

Budgets

12 Read Texts A and B and answer the questions.

1 Which budget description asks for more money than they already have?
2 In which example is the way of spending money expressed more clearly?
3 Which is more likely to influence a positive decision about funding a project? Why?

A

> We seek £50,000 as funds to support the Education for the Disabled Youth Programme. With your assistance, we will be able to help 25 disabled students to attend A-level classes and to send 25 more to college. We believe that providing educational programmes to all qualified disabled students will help in the economic growth of our county.

B

> Our institution is requesting $18,000 from the Help Fund to support this program that makes a meaningful difference in the lives of our youth. A contribution from our partners accounts for $10,000 that will give us initial support and cover salary expenses.

13 In Texts A and B, underline words/phrases which help to describe the budget for an intended project. Why do you think the active voice is used here?

14 Study the Language Support box below. Substitute the words/phrases you underlined in Texts A and B with those from the Language Support box.

> **Language Support: budgets**
>
> We seek / are seeking … (sum of money) to … (to support …).
> We request / are requesting … (sum of money) from …
> … is intended to fund … (the staff positions) and provide … (facilities).
> The grant request is for funding for … (a period of time).
> Partners contribute … to the project.
> The applicant is covering (salary / travelling) costs.

15 Suggest improvements for the less successful budget description from Activity 12.

16 Add information about the budget to the executive summary of your project. Use the Language Support box in Activity 14 to help you.

17 Combine all the parts of the executive summary you have written and finalise it, paying attention to its structure and style.

Have you …

- used formal language?
- given your project a title?
- given contact person information?
- presented the mission of your organisation?
- identified the main problem and your needs?

- described your project in brief?
- included expected results?
- stated the budget needed for your project?
- checked the grammar, spelling and punctuation?

18 Work in groups. Think about your joint research project and write an executive summary of a grant proposal in order to get funding.

Unit 5 Describing visual data

By the end of this unit you will be able to

➡ identify the features of descriptions of visual information

➡ refer to visuals

➡ interpret visuals

➡ write a short description of trends

Lesson 1 Visual information

Lead-in

1 Work in pairs and discuss the questions.

1 What visuals are usually used by scientists in your field to present data?
2 If you use visuals in research papers, do you use them extensively or only for certain aspects? Why? / Why not?

Types of visual

2 Match visuals 1–6 with illustrations a–f.

1 a histogram
2 a bar chart
3 a line graph
4 a table
5 a scatter plot
6 a pie chart

a _____

Tasks completed	Before experiment (%)	After experiment (%)
Bachelor's students	13.6	43.4
Master's students	15.7	87.6

b _____

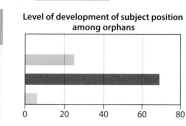

Level of development of subject position among orphans

low
medium
high

c _____

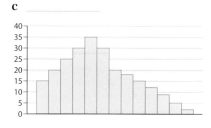

d _____

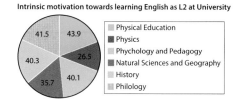

Intrinsic motivation towards learning English as L2 at University

Physical Education
Physics
Phychology and Pedagogy
Natural Sciences and Geography
History
Philology

e _____

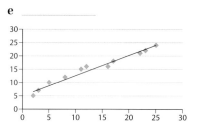

f _____

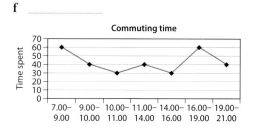

Commuting time

3 Match the types of visuals a–f with the purpose they are used for in academic texts.

a a histogram
b a bar chart
c a line graph

d a table
e a scatter plot
f a pie chart

1 A _____ is used to show exact numbers.
2 A _____ is used to display relations between items.
3 A _____ or _____ are used to show trends.
4 A _____ is used to show proportions of a whole.
5 A _____ is used to investigate the possible relationship between two variables that both relate to the same 'event'.

Features of descriptions of visual information

4 Work in pairs. Look at the histogram below and describe it. Do you know the percentage of women researchers in your country?

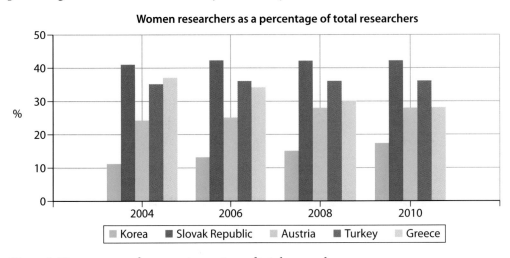

Figure 1. Women researchers as a percentage of total researchers.

5 Read the description below of the histogram. Which sentence (1–6):

a refers to specific information in the diagram? ____
b adds some details? ____
c summarises the main findings? ____
d makes a reference to the histogram? ____
e makes a prediction? ____
f introduces the main findings? ____

¹The chart in Figure 1 shows the number of women researchers in five OECD countries. ²The vertical Y-axis illustrates a percentage of female researchers; the horizontal X-axis presents a time period from 2004 to 2010. ³It can be clearly seen that the figures for all countries has remained relatively stable with some fluctuations between approximately 11% in Korea in 2004 and 42% in the Slovak Republic in 2010. ⁴It also demonstrates that in two of the countries, the number of female researchers has not changed. ⁵In general, countries experienced no dramatic changes in the rates of women researchers. ⁶If the trend continues, we may expect an overall increase in the number of women involved in research.

6 Complete the table with phrases from the description which are used to refer to visual information and to interpret it.

referring to a visual	interpreting a visual
The chart in Figure 1 shows ...	*... remained stable*

7 Read the phrases below. Say what they are used for in a description of visual information.

- As shown in (Figure 1, Table 2, etc.) ...
- The diagram outlines ...
- The figure above/below illustrates ...
- The pie chart represents ...
- The line graph depicts/indicates ...

8 Look again at Figure 1 in Activity 4. Complete each sentence below with the name of the country.

1 In _____ , figures continued to rise slowly and reached almost 20% in 2010.

2 In _____ and _____ , the trend remained almost unchanged at over 40% and 35% respectively.

3 _____ proved to be the country with the highest rate of women researchers, at approximately 41% in 2004 and 42% in 2010.

4 The rates in _____ were consistently the lowest, which is half of that of _____ .

5 The figures for women researchers in _____ grew slowly from about 23% in 2004 and they stabilised at around 28% in 2008 and 2010.

6 Throughout the whole period, rates in _____ remained stable at around 25%, which put the country in a mid-position between Korea and the Slovak Republic and _____ .

7 _____ , however, appeared to be the only country with a steady downward trend, from approximately 35% of women researchers in 2004 to slightly less than 30% in 2010.

9 Add phrases to the description in Activity 8 which help to refer to visuals. Then underline phases which interpret visual information from the histogram.

Lesson 2 Writing about trends

Lead-in

1 **Work in pairs and discuss these questions.**

1 In which fields of study do researchers need to describe trends or changes?

2 What type of visual would you choose if you had to describe trends and changes in your field?

Basic trends

2 **Study Figure 2 and say which type of visit to the UK is the most popular.**

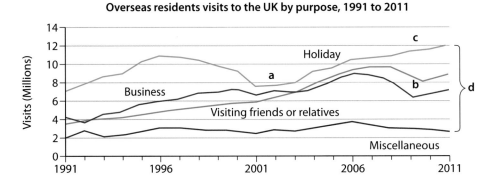

Figure 2. Overseas residents visits to the UK by purpose, 1991 to 2011

3 **Read the description below and match sentences 1–4 to parts a–d in Figure 2.**

This line graph in Figure 2 shows the number of overseas residents visits to the UK between 1991 and 2011. ¹As shown in the graph, there has been a gradual increase in visits. ²However, there was a slight decline in 2001. It is obvious that visits for each of the main purposes of visit (holiday, business and to visit friends or relatives) all rose in 2011. ³In 2011, the number of holiday visits grew by 2.9% to 12 million. ⁴The number of visits to the UK for business and visiting friends or relatives fell between 2006 and 2010. These types of visit showed an increase in 2011.

4 **In the text in Activity 3, underline words and phrases which describe trends. Find words and expressions with the same idea in the Language Support box.**

Language Support: describing trends

	slight gradual steady considerable sharp dramatic rapid	increase growth rise decrease decline drop fall	*with a definite period of time*: from (*July*) to (*September*). during (*March*). between (*2005*) and (*2012*).
There was a (very)			
	noticeable considerable	fluctuation	
Results, prices, numbers, etc.	increased grew rose decreased declined dropped fell	insignificantly slightly gradually steadily sharply dramatically rapidly	
	fluctuated	considerably	

5 Rewrite sentences 1–4 from the text in Activity 3, using words/phrases from the Language Support box and the prompts below.

1 As shown in the graph, the number of visits has _____ .
2 However, they _____ _____ in 2001.
3 In 2011, _____ _____ a 2.9% _____ to 12.0 million in the number of holiday visits.
4 Between 2006 and 2010 _____ _____ a _____ in the visits to the UK for business and visiting friends or relatives.

Writing a short description of trends

6 Look at the graph below, then complete the sentences. In some sentences, more than one answer is possible.

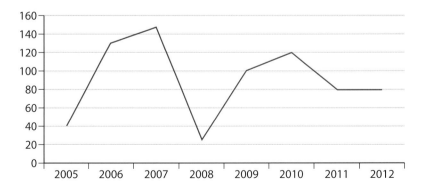

Figure 3. Articles submitted to international journals

The line graph in ¹_____ shows the number of ²_____ submitted to different international journals by researchers from our institution ³_____ 2005 and ⁴_____ . First, the number of articles ⁵_____ sharply from 2005 ⁶_____ 2006. Then, as you can see, it increased ⁷_____ between 2006 and 2007. Clearly, the number of articles reached its peak in ⁸_____ . There was a sharp ⁹_____ in 2008. After this, we experienced gradual ¹⁰_____ . From the middle of 2011, the number of articles remained ¹¹_____ .

7 Make a diagram showing trends or changes, and describe it in 100–120 words.

8 Work in pairs. Take turns to listen to each other's description and draw it. Then compare your diagram with the original.

9 Read your partner's original description. Which of the following did they do?

- referred to relevant visual information in the diagram
- drew the reader's attention to the important features
- summarised the most important trends or changes
- used linking words to make the description coherent
- wrote the description in a formal style

Academic vocabulary

Abbreviations: n = noun / pl n = plural noun;
vi = intransitive verb; vt = transitive verb
adj = adjective; adv = adverb; conj = conjunction;
phr = phrase; phr v = phrasal verb;
abb = abbreviation.

A

abstract *n* (Reading, Unit 3, Lesson 1; Writing, Unit 3, Lesson 1) a shortened form of a speech, article, book, etc., giving only the most important facts or ideas

across disciplines *phr* (Listening, Unit 4, Lesson 2) in all disciplines

acknowledge *vt* (Reading, Unit 3, Lesson 3) to accept, admit or recognise something, or the truth or existence of something

address *vt* (Reading, Unit 2, Lesson 3) to give attention to or deal with a matter or problem

advance *vt* (Reading, Unit 2, Lesson 3) to go or move something forward, or to develop or improve something

applied *adj* (Reading, Unit 2, Lesson 3) relating to a subject of study, especially a science, that has a practical use, e.g. *pure and applied mathematics/science*

apply *phr v* (Listening, Unit 4, Lesson 4) to use something, for example, a law in a particular situation

apply for *vt* (Writing, Unit 1, Lesson 1) to request something, usually officially, especially in writing or sending a form

approximately *adv* (Writing, Unit 5, Lesson 1) more or less; not exactly

assess *vt* (Reading, Unit 3, Lesson 2) to judge or decide the amount, value, quality or importance of something

associated (with) *adj* (Writing, Unit 1, Lesson 3) be connected to

assume *vi* (Writing, Unit 2, Unit 3, Lesson 2) to think that something is likely to be true, although you have no proof

assumption *n* (Writing, Unit 3, Lesson 1) something that you think is true without having any proof

attempt *vi* (Listening, Unit 4, Lesson 1) to try to do something, especially something difficult

axis *n* (Writing, Unit 5, Lesson 1) a line or a graph used to show a position of a point

B

background *n* (Writing, Unit 3, Lesson 1) the situation that an event happens in, or things which have happened in the past which affect it

bar chart *n* (Writing, Unit 5, Lesson 1) a mathematical picture in which different amounts are represented by thin vertical or horizontal rectangles which have the same width but different heights or lengths

body *n* (Listening, Unit 4, Lesson 4) a large amount of something

C

call for papers *phr* (Reading, Unit 1, Lesson 2) a formal invitation to give a lecture or present new research at a conference

case study *n* (Listening, Unit 3, Lesson 2) a detailed account giving information about the development of a person, group, or thing, especially in order to show general principles

claim *vi* (Reading, Unit 3, Lesson 3; Writing, Unit 2, Lesson 1) 1. to say that something is true, although you have not proved it; 2. to say that you have done or achieved something

clarification *n* (Listening, Unit 3, Lesson 3) an explanation or more details that makes something clear or easier to understand

collaborate *vi* (Reading, Unit 2, Lesson 2) to work with someone else for a special purpose

combine (with) *vt* (Writing, Unit 4, Lesson 2) 1. to exist together, or to join together to make a single thing or group; 2. to do two activities at the same time

concise *adj* (Reading, Unit 1, Lesson 2) giving a lot of information clearly in a few words

conclusion *n* (Writing, Unit 1, Lesson 2; Unit 3, Lesson 1) the opinion you have after considering all the information about something

conduct *vt* (Reading, Unit 3, Lesson 3; Writing, Unit 1, Lesson 3; Unit 2, Lesson 1) to organise and perform a particular activity, e.g. an experiment

consistent *adj* (Reading, Unit 3, Lesson 3) always behaving or happening in a similar, especially positive, way

contribute *vt* (Writing, Unit 4, Lesson 2) to give something in order to provide or achieve something together with other people

correlation (between) *n* (Reading, Unit 3, Lesson 2) a connection or relationship between two or more facts, numbers, etc.

correspond *vi* (Writing, Unit 4, Lesson 1) to match or be similar or equal

credibility *n* (Reading, Unit 4, Lesson 2) the fact that something can be believed or trusted

criterion *n* often *pl* **criteria** (Reading, Unit 2, Lesson 2) a standard by which you judge, decide about or deal with something

critical *adj* (Reading, Unit 1, Lesson 3) of the greatest importance to the way things might happen

crucial *adj* (Reading, Unit 4, Lesson 1) extremely important or necessary

cutting edge *adj* (Reading, Unit 1, Lesson 1; Unit 2, Lesson 1) very modern and with all the newest features

D

data *pl n* (Writing, Unit 5, Lesson 1; Listening, Unit 4, Lesson 2) information from research or a **survey**

deadline *n* (Reading, Unit 1, Lesson 1) a time or day by which something must be done, e.g. *an abstract submission deadline*

decline *vi* (Writing Unit 5, Lesson 2) to become less, worse or lower

define *vt* (Listening, Unit 4, Lesson 1) to explain and describe the meaning and exact limits of something

degree *n* (Reading, Unit 1, Lesson 3; Unit 2, Lesson 1) a course of study at a college or university, or the qualification given to a student who has done this course, e.g. BA, MA, PhD, etc.

demonstrate *vt/vi* (Writing, Unit 2, Lesson 1) to show or prove that something exists or is true

digital pointer *n* (Listening, Unit 2, Lesson 2) an object you use to point at something that is using an electronic system that changes images into signals in the form of numbers before it stores them or sends them

dimension *n* (Listening, Unit 4, Lesson 1) a measurement of something in a particular direction, especially its height, length, or width

discipline *n* (Reading, Unit 2, Lesson 1) a particular area of study, especially a subject studied at a college or university

dissemination *n* (Reading, Unit 4, Lesson 2) spreading or giving out to a lot of people, e.g. *dissemination of research results*

E

e-conference *n* (Reading, Unit 1, Lesson 3) a conference held online

educational platform *n* (Reading, Unit 2, Lesson 2) web-based software designed to manage the organisation of a course of study

e-learning *n* (Reading, Unit 1, Lesson 1; Unit 2, Lesson 2; Listening, Unit 3, Lesson 2) learning done by studying at home, using computers and courses delivered via the Internet

emphasise *vt* (Reading, Unit 2, Lesson 3; Writing, Unit 2, Lesson 1; Speaking, Unit 2, Lesson 1) to make something clearer

empirical *adj* (Reading, Unit 3, Lesson 1) based on what is experienced or seen, rather than on theory

enhance *vt* (Writing, Unit 4, Lesson 1) to improve the quality, amount or strength of something

enrol *vi* (Reading, Unit 2, Lesson 2) to put yourself or someone else onto the official list of members of a course, college or group

equal opportunity *n* *often pl* **opportunities** (Reading, Unit 4, Lesson 1) the principle of treating all people the same, and not being influenced by a person's sex, race, religion, etc.

escalate *vi* (Writing, Unit 3, Lesson 1) to become greater or more serious

ethics usually *pl* (Reading, Unit 4, Lesson 2) a system of accepted beliefs that control behaviour, e.g. *research ethics*

evidence *n* (Listening, Unit 4, Lesson 2) one or more reasons for believing that something is or is not true

executive summary *n* (Writing, Unit 4, Lesson 1) a document that gives the main points of a detailed report, usually provided at the beginning of the report

explore *vt* (Writing, Unit 3, Lesson 1; Unit 3, Lesson 2) to search and discover about something

express (*vt***) an opinion** (Listening, Unit 3, Lesson 3) give one's opinion on something

extension lead *n* (Listening, Unit 2, Lesson 1) an extra wire used to take electricity to a piece of electrical equipment when it is an extra distance from the nearest socket

extensive *adj* (Writing, Unit 4, Lesson 1) covering a large area, having a great range

F

facilities *pl n* (Listening, Unit 1, Lesson 2, Unit 1, Lesson 3; Writing, Unit 4, Lesson 2; Reading, Unit 1, Lesson 2) the buildings, equipment and services provided for a particular purpose

feasibility *n* (Reading, Unit 4, Lesson 2) whether something can be made, done, or achieved, or is reasonable

feedback *n* (Listening, Unit 3, Lesson 4; Writing, Unit 1, Lesson 3) information or statements of opinion about something, such as a new product, that can tell you if it is successful or liked

finding *n often pl* **findings** (Reading, Unit 3, Lesson 1) a piece (or pieces) of information that is discovered during an official examination of a problem, situation or object

forum *n* (Reading, Unit 1, Lesson 1; Unit 1, Lesson 3) a situation or meeting in which people can talk about a problem or matter especially of public interest, e.g. *an academic forum*

foster *vi* (Reading, Unit 1, Lesson 1; Unit 4, Lesson 1) to encourage the development or growth of ideas or feelings

funding *n* (Writing, Unit 4, Lesson 1; Unit 4, Lesson 2) money given by a government or an organisation for an event or activity

G

grant *n* (Reading, Unit 4, Lesson 1) an amount of money given especially by the government to a person or organisation for a special purpose, e.g. *a student/ research grant*

H

histogram *n* (Writing, Unit 5) a bar chart/graph

host organisation *n* (Reading, Unit 4, Lesson 2) institution that holds an event

Humanities *n pl* (Reading, Unit 2, Lesson 1) subjects such as literature, language, history and philosophy

hypothesis *n pl* **hypotheses** (Writing, Unit 3, Lesson 1; Listening, Unit 4, Lesson 2) a suggested explanation for something which has not yet been proved to be true

I

identify *vt* (Writing, Unit 4, Lesson 1) to recognise a problem, need or fact

illustrate *vt* (Writing, Unit 3, Lesson 1) to give more information or examples to explain or prove something

impact *vt* (Writing, Unit 3, Lesson 1) to have an effect on

implication *n* (Writing, Unit 3, Lesson 1) the effect that an action or a decision will have on something else in the future

implement *vt* (Writing, Unit 1, Lesson 3; Unit 4, Lesson 1) to start using a plan or system

increase *vi* (Writing, Unit 4, Lesson 1; Unit 5, Lesson 1) to become greater in size or larger in amount

indicate *vt/vi* (Writing, Unit 3, Lesson 1) to show, point, make clear

interaction *n* (Reading, Unit 1, Lesson 3; Unit 2, Lesson 1) when two or more people or things communicate with or react to each other, e.g. *interaction between students and the teacher*

interdisciplinary *adj* (Reading, Unit 1, Lesson 1) involving two or more different subjects or areas of knowledge, e.g. *interdisciplinary research*

interrelated *adj* (Writing, Unit 3, Lesson 1) connected in such a way that each thing has an effect on or depends on the other

invest *vt* (Writing, Unit 4, Lesson 1) to put money, effort, time, etc. into something to make a profit or get an advantage

J

journal *n* (Reading, Unit 3, Lesson 1) a serious magazine which is published regularly, usually about a specialist subject

K

keynote speaker *n* (Reading, Unit 1, Lesson 2) the person who gives the main presentation at a conference

L

launch *n* (Reading, Unit 2, Lesson 1) to begin something such as a plan or introduce something new such as a product

learning performance *n* (Listening, Unit 3, Lesson 2) how well a person learns

line graph *n* (Writing, Unit 5, Lesson 1) a drawing that uses lines to show how different pieces of information are related to each other

M

make an impact on/in *phr* (Reading, Unit 2, Lesson 2) have a powerful effect on a situation or person

make predictions *phr* (Writing, Unit 4, Lesson 2; Listening, Unit 1, Lesson 1) to make a statement about what you think will happen in the future

meet expectations *phr* (Reading, Unit 2, Lesson 1) satisfy standards or hopes

multidisciplinary *adj* (Reading, Unit 2, Lesson 3) relating to or involving people from different types of work or who have different types of knowledge

N

Natural Sciences *n* (Reading, Unit 2, Lesson 1) pure sciences such as biology, physics and chemistry

O

objective *n* (Writing, Unit 3, Lesson 1) something that you plan to do or achieve

object (of research) *n* (Listening, Unit 4, Lesson 2) a thing or a phenomenon that is researched

OSS *abb* (Reading, Unit 2, Lesson 2) open source software

outcome *n* (Writing, Unit 2, Lesson 2) a result or effect of an action, situation

overview *n* (Listening, Unit 4, Lesson 1) a short description of something that provides general information about it, but no details

P

panel *n* (Reading, Unit 1, Lesson 2) a small group of people chosen to give advice, make a decision, or publicly discuss their opinions as entertainment, e.g. *a panel session*

peer review *n* (Reading, Unit 3, Lesson 1) a system in which people you work with report on your performance so that you and your managers know areas that you need to improve, or an occasion when this happens

persistent *adj* (Listening, Unit 3, Lesson 4) lasting for a long time or difficult to get rid of

pie chart *n* (Writing, Unit 5, Lesson 1) a circle divided into several parts to represent how the total amount of something is divided up

plenary *adj* (Reading, Unit 1, Lesson 3) describes a meeting at which all the members of a group or organisation are present, especially at a conference

plug in *phr v* (Listening, Unit 2, Lesson 1) to attach electrical equipment to a supply of electricity with a plug

predict *vt/vi* (Writing, Unit 3, Lesson 1) to say what you think will happen in the future

prediction *n* (Writing, Unit 3, Lesson 1) when you say what you think will happen in the future

project development *n* (Listening, Unit 3, Lesson 2) the process of creating a project

proposal *n* (Writing, Unit 1, Lesson 3; Unit 1, Lesson 4; Reading, Unit 1, Lesson 2) a suggestion, often a written one, e.g. *conference proposal*

propose *vt/vi* (Writing, Unit 4, Lesson 1) to offer or suggest a possible plan or action for other people to consider

Q

qualitative *adj* (of research) (Writing, Unit 3, Lesson 1) relating to how good something is, usually based on empirical data

query *n* (Writing, Unit 1, Lesson 3) a question about a situation or fact, often to someone in authority

questionnaire *n* (Reading, Unit 3, Lesson 2) a list of questions that several people are asked so that information can be collected about something

quote *vt* (Listening, Unit 4, Lesson 4) to repeat the words that someone else has said or written

R

reboot *vt* (Listening, Unit 2, Lesson 1) if you reboot a computer, or if a computer reboots, you switch it off and then switch it on again a short time later, especially in order to get rid of a problem or after you have put new software onto the computer

reliable *adj* (Reading, Unit 3, Lesson 3) something or someone that is reliable can be trusted or believed because they work or behave well in the way you expect

respondent *n* (Reading, Unit 2, Lesson 3; Unit 3, Lesson 3) a person who answers a request for information

review *n* (Reading, Unit 3, Lesson 1) the act of considering something again in order to make changes to it, give an opinion on it or study it

round table *n* (Reading, Unit 1, Lesson 3) *a round-table discussion/meeting* is one where people meet and talk in conditions of equality